NIGHT CITY

Where to Drink and Party After Work and After Hours

TOKYO NIGHT CITY

Where to Drink and Party After Work and After Hours

**Jude
Brand**

Charles E. Tuttle Company
Rutland, Vermont and Tokyo, Japan

This book is dedicated to my liver

The information in this book was checked as thoroughly as possible before going to press. The publisher accepts no responsibility for any changes that have occurred since, nor for any variance of fact from that recorded here in good faith by the author.

All photographs taken by and copyright of the author.

Published by the Charles E. Tuttle Company, Inc.
of Rutland, Vermont & Tokyo, Japan
with editorial offices at
2-6 Suido 1-chome, Bunkyo-ku, Tokyo 112

Library of Congress Catalog Card No. 93-60060
International Standard Book No. 0-8048-1896-7

First edition, 1993

Printed in Japan

Contents

Plates following page 72: Wired; Fare game;
Infinity within; Deep; Body con; The vibe
meisters; Hi lite; and Life's a drag

Acknowledgments

Hard-earned thanks go to Piotr Podworski and Sandro Klein, two indestructable party boys who partied hard with me and managed to keep up most nights. I would also like to thank the following people who took me places, gave me tips, or threw me freebies: Kieran Daly, Torin Boyd, Charlie Parisek, Don Morton, Bryan Harrell, Steve Herman, Bill Hersey, Kenny Abrahams, Johnathan McDowell, Monday Michiru Akiyoshi, Snezana, Gary Callicot, Monica Grab, Mike Cline, Joarie, Brad and the boys from The Hitmen, Johan Engblom, Laura Hanifin, Eric Kelso, Rick Kennedy, Georgina Pope, Tom Conrad, Philip Sandoz, Mark Schilling, Muramasa Kudo, Bobby Ettienne, Alison Panamaroff, Bernie Warrell, JD Wilson, Mayumi Nakazawa, Bernard Ryan, Ma-chan, Anya Block, Vincent Young Jones, Corky Alexander, Momoko Saito, Will (Piotr's friend), Shogo Watanabe, Ralph Cassell, and Titus Boeder.

Additional thanks go to my photography teachers David Wade and Tim Porter, who taught me that an f-stop is not an expletive and provided endless instruction and support, and to Kato and Togashi at National Photo, who created excellent-quality reproduction prints of my photographs for this book.

For computer-related support I must thank Richard Keirstead, Adi Computer (Indonesia), Jim Merk, Dennis Davis, Malcolm Sullivan, and Johan, Gilles, and Zebastian.

Introduction

There are literally hundreds of thousands of bars and clubs in Tokyo. Finding your way through this maze can either be delightfully entertaining or irritatingly frustrating. This volume maximizes your chances of finding what you want and helps to eliminate expensive mistakes. *Tokyo Night City* offers a comprehensive overview of the nightlife in this city, describes over 100 establishments in detail, tells you what to expect, and shows you how to get there.

Tokyo is full of diversity and subcultures. Since the push for internationalization that emerged during the last decade or so, the range of nightlife available has become even more varied. Now, in addition to the omnipresent *nomiya* and the exorbitantly expensive hostess club, there are also hundreds of Western-style bars and clubs. By Western I don't mean exact replicas. They are based on a Western concept which has then been reinterpreted to create bars like nowhere else in the world. They are not all new either. Some of them have been around for years, like Lupin, which opened in 1928.

The difference between traditional Japanese drinking establishments and these newer offshoots is pretty simple. In a typical *nomiya* or hostess club your enjoyment as a customer is based on your relationship with the *mama*, *master*, or other member of staff and not so much on your interaction with other customers. But in Western-style bars it is OK to interact as well.

Introduction

There are now hundreds of these new-era bars but the network of *nomiya* honeycombing through the city accounts for the thousands in the overall nightspot figure. Because there are so many traditional drinking spots and because your enjoyment of them ends up being so personal, it's up to you to find the best one near your home. But I have included some irresistible little *nomiya* and the odd hostess club because they have a curious appeal outside their usual realm.

The purpose of this book is to provide entertainment alternatives. No two partiers are alike and every individual has different moods, so I have covered as wide a variety of clubs as possible. As I made my way through Tokyo's previously unmapped night city labyrinth, various groupings of clubs became apparent. These were jazz venues, discos and dance clubs, Latin and reggae bars, *gaijin* bars, gay and lesbian bars, low-key bars patronized mainly by Japanese, and other hard-to-categorize or one-off establishments. These groupings became the seven chapters of this book: All That Jazz, Dance and Prance, Ethnobop, Gaijin Ghetto, Les Girls and Boys, Mellow Yellow, and Wild Cards. An overview of each scene and an outline of what to expect appears at the beginning of each chapter. There are also two appendixes, one covering Yokohama and the other where to eat late.

The night map of a city always changes more rapidly than its day grid. Descriptions of the clubs listed in these pages will start changing even as the book is being printed. Keep in mind that the names and faces of bars may change, but something usually takes their place. Roppongi will always be relatively easy to plug into, but if that party mecca doesn't satisfy your needs, this book will allow you to find what you want. To keep on top of the turnover of information, regular updates are mandatory and already scheduled for publication.

Each page features a description of the club, lists its hours of operation, address, phone number, and a yen symbol to rate the initial cash outlay necessary to get a drink. ¥ means that your first drink will cost you up to or the equivalent of ¥1,000, ¥¥ means that it will cost you more than ¥1,000 but no more than ¥2,000, and so on. Dance clubs and venues with a cover charge that sometimes include drinks have also been rated according to your initial outlay. If it is ¥3,000 to get in but you get two drinks, it's still going to cost you ¥3,000 to get the first one, so it rates ¥¥¥.

In addition to the above information, each page features a walking map to the club from the closest train station. Symbols used in the maps are:

Ⓢ for the closest subway exit

[GS] for a gas station

[K] for a *koban*, a neighborhood police station

卍 for a temple or shrine

★ for the location of the club

Japanese words and English words with specialized local meanings have been italicized and explained in the glossary.

So, get out there and grab a thread and follow it through the night city. See you there.

All That Jazz

Japan has embraced jazz like no other genre of Western music. Interest has existed here since the 20s, after which it steadily developed to generate a soft jazz boom during the big-band, dance-hall days of the 30s. Popularity continued to grow during the American Occupation, when the USO were the first to bring such stars as Benny Goodman to Japan to entertain their enlisted personnel. The Officers' Club was the only place to catch these acts until the advent of luxury nightclubs like the New Latin Quarter and the Copa Cabana. Many American musicians who found themselves working for Uncle Sam began teaching local artists how to play. The first major wave of jazz was breaking across Japan, but toward the end of the 50s the dance-hall days were dying. Big bands were crumbling into small combos whose playing styles were evolving into bee-bop and beyond.

By the 60s jazz was developing a new image in Japan. At the beginning of the decade it was lumped in with pop, country and western, and even Hawaiian music. It was at this time that Oscar Peterson invited Toshiko Akiyoshi to study jazz piano at Berkeley. She in turn invited Sadao Watanabe. Toward the end of the decade the first pure jazz clubs were opening— some big and fancy, some small and dirty. Watanabe returned to Japan to teach modern jazz workshops, which were popular with younger people and led more local musicians to form their own groups. This

All That Jazz

paved the way for the second wave in Japan, but this time it was modern jazz that swept through the scene. At the same time that America's youth was preaching free love and draft dodging, there was an equivalent social, cultural, and intellectual rethinking in Japan. Jazz had taken on the dimensions of an esoteric youth movement. It was mostly snubbed by the establishment, but imensely popular with freedom thinkers. Anyone you meet who was here then will tell you that it was wild. Customs officials were still relatively naive so a lot of drugs made it onto the scene. All the big names and their entourages were touring Japan. Eventually someone was caught and immigration started cracking down on visas for musicians.

By the 70s jazz had become big business and, therefore, part of the establishment again. The first large outdoor festivals were organized and more mainstream, luxury clubs were opening. By the 1980s, however, interest had started to wane. The audience was aging and younger people just weren't taking their place. Before the recent emergence of acid-jazz and jazz-rap, the genre had waited many years to exert an influence (beyond history) on current musical styles. Venues now tend to be extremely up-market and a little too sanitized. It is also hard for young people to afford an interest, as serious amounts of money can change hands for an enthusiast to buy the privilege of simply entering a club.

Pia features comprehensive schedules for venues which will be valuable once you know the musicians. The clubs listed here will help you get to know them.

Body and Soul

Kyoko Seiki recently relocated her snazzy little jazz club in the basement of a brand-new building right around the corner from one of her major competitors, Blue Note. The addition of this club on this block in Aoyama effectively creates a mini jazz village, offering both a high and low-end venue. Body and Soul is low end in terms of cost. The reasonably-priced cover charge does not include any drinks, but unlike Blue Note, it does entitle you stay all night. The lighting is subdued and the interior is sophisticated, solid, and unscuffed (except for one panel taken from the *mama*'s previous venue which was signed by some of the club's more famous performers). The stage area is surrounded by tables and chairs which are backed by a bar with high stools and a balcony with more tables and chairs. These seating levels are tiered so that everyone has a good view. The *mama* is as vigilant as a Ginza hostess in administering to her regular customers, but the overall atmosphere is pretty loose.

Open from 6:30 p.m. till 12 a.m.
Monday to Saturday. First set at
8 p.m. Closed on Sunday.
Anise Minami-aoyama Bldg.
B1F,
6-13-9 Minami-aoyama,
Minato-ku.
(03) 5466-3348
¥¥¥¥

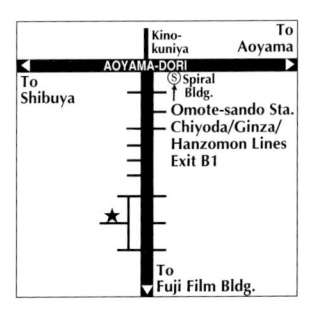

Blue Note

Meanwhile on the high end of the scene, customers at this venue are being scalped ¥8,000 plus at the door for the pleasure of plugging into a one-hour set. This hefty cover charge does not include drinks. The club features only famous overseas acts and equally famous local ones. Many jazz buffs will go to this venue only if these stars are not playing at another more reasonably-priced venue. The management says they can't make it any cheaper—the New York club costs US$40 (around ¥5,000) anyway. Because the sets are so short and the entry entitles you to only one, this venue is possibly best used for catching vocalists. Instrument-led groups are just starting to cook at the end of an hour, which can be frustrating for both the audience and the act. The interior is spacious and airy with a sunken seating area faced by an elevated stage. All the walls are mirrored and every seat is good. Even if you get stuck behind someone with a bouffant hairdo, you will have a good view of the stage.

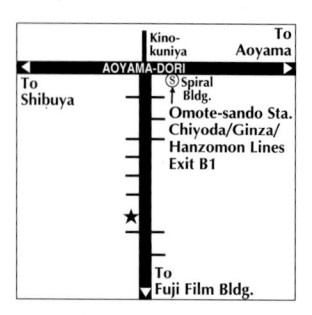

Open from 6 p.m. till 2 a.m. Monday to Saturday. First set at 7:30 p.m. Closed on Sunday. FIK Bldg. B1F, 5-13-3 Minami-aoyama, Minato-ku. (03) 3407-5781 ¥¥¥¥¥¥¥¥+

G•H Nine

This is a subdued and sophisticated jazz spot delivering a mixed bag of local acts for less than you would be scalped for in other better-known clubs. It is definitely worth the effort to make your way to Ueno if you don't already live or work in the area. The club is located directly under the glass pyramid which gives the Uno Building its distinctive look, but which makes heating a little difficult during winter. It consists of a main floor and mezzanine, which are connected by a slightly wobbly metal staircase. You must be seated to watch the show, but with three sets throughout the night, the turnover of tables seems to accommodate everyone interested. Reservations would be advised for more popular acts. If you're really unlucky and can't get a seat, the building's first floor coffee shop shows a large screen simulcast of what's going on upstairs. They serve stylish-looking cocktails but fairly average beers, with only Grolsch to break the monotony. Food is also available.

Open from 6 p.m. till 12 a.m.
every night. First set at 7 p.m.
Uno Bldg. 9F,
4-4-6 Ueno,
Taito-ku.
(03) 3837-2525
¥¥

Vagabond

A reassuringly-solid central staircase fashioned from heavy wooden banisters forms the entrance to this poky jazz club. Upstairs, the walls are covered with an assortment of posters and paintings, the ceiling is hung with a jumble of potted plants and dried flowers, the lightshades are draped with lace doilies, and old brass fixtures from railway carriages serve as bag racks. The retro nature of all these decorations and the overwhelming feeling of claustrophobia from being crammed in among all this stuff, make you feel like you've stumbled into your grandmother's parlor. It is a fabulously atmospheric environment in which to sit and sip and listen to some classic skat and blues, or bring some friends and make a night of it. The piano, the back of which juts out precariously over the stairwell, is dusted off every evening from seven p.m. (after which it will be impossible to get a seat) to deliver some suitably lethargic jazz standards. They also feature a basic *yakitoriya* style menu.

Open from 5:30 p.m. till 11:30 p.m. Monday to Saturday, till 10:30 p.m. on Sunday, and till 11 p.m. on holidays.
1-4-20 Nishi-shinjuku 2F, Shinjuku-ku.
(03) 3348-9109
¥

Pit Inn

Pit Inn is almost a synonym for jazz in Tokyo. The Roppongi and Shinjuku venues have been serving the local jazz community for more than two decades. The interior of the Roppongi one is spacious, but quickly fills up when the club's more popular acts take the spotlight. Latecomers may be forced to stand or be jammed behind a pillar with zero visibility. Everyone stops talking and pays excruciatingly silent attention when the band kicks in. At this one they feature a mixed bag of jazz genres, including pop and fusion. The Shinjuku Pit Inn recently moved to the basement of a new building, leaving many punters sad that the older, more-settled club has gone. This one features only jazz, which can be taken very seriously by those who say they enjoy it. The audiences in both clubs are a little too well behaved for my liking. If you want to start researching the local jazz scene, however, either of these clubs would be an excellent place to start.

Roppongi: *Open from 6:30 p.m. till 10:30 p.m. every day. First set at 7:30 p.m. Shimei Bldg. B1F, 3-17-7 Roppongi, Minato-ku. (03) 3585-1063 ¥¥¥¥*

Shinjuku: *Open from 7 p.m. till 10:30 p.m. every day. First set at 7:30 p.m. Acord Bldg. B1F, 2-12-4 Shinjuku, Shinjuku-ku. (03) 3354-2024 ¥¥¥¥*

All That Jazz

Aketa

You can wander into this jazz venue on any night and find a dedicated group of musicians delivering high-quality jazz. The owner, Aketagawa-san, started out during the modern jazz wave of the 60s and is now a well-known personality and musician on the scene. He is basically one of the lads, because of which his club is firmly plugged into the local circuit. One third of his bar's tiny interior is given over to a stage and the rest is crammed with coffee tables and padded chairs, all of which face the band. The only real interior detail is a colorful, modern mural which creates a fresh, inspirational backdrop for the performers. Once you know who's who on the scene, this would be an excellent low-profile, low-budget venue in which to catch a favorite act. If you're just starting out, you can rely on hearing excellent-quality jazz in whatever style the band is playing. The audience is fairly relaxed, yet respectful, but this will vary according to the act. Definitely worth a visit.

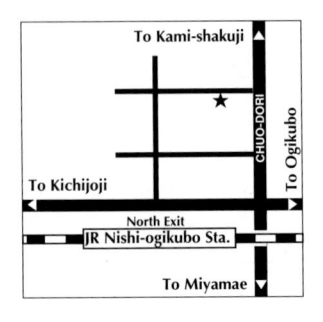

Open from 7 p.m. till 11 p.m. Sunday to Monday and till 2 a.m. on Saturday. Sometimes a cheap 3 p.m. matinee on Sunday. Yoshino Bldg. B1F, 3-21-13 Nishi-ogikita, Suginami-ku. (03) 3395-9507 ¥¥/¥¥¥

Jirokichi

This is a truly inspiring little jazz, soul, funk, and blues venue right in the heart of Koenji. You can wander in on almost any night and find some eccentric Japanese musician hammering out a tune from one of the genres listed above. A lot of foreigners live in this area and many of them patronize this club. While the Japanese clientele may idle into sit-and-listen mode, some *gaijin* enthusiasts will also usually wander in and automatically seed the atmosphere with a more animated mood. Once the locals realize that it is acceptable to have fun in the face of jazz, they usually loosen up as well. The Japanese who live in the area have already been exposed to liberal doses of foreign tastes and attitudes, and tend to be cooler anyway. This is definitely one jazz venue where it is OK to party. Once a month you can catch an all-night blues session which kicks in early and stays cooking late. With very friendly staff and a very reasonable cover charge, this venue is definitely worth a look.

Open from 5:30 p.m. till 2 a.m.
Tuesday to Sunday. Closed on
Monday.
Koenji Bldg. B1F,
2-3-4 Kita-koenji,
Suginami-ku.
(03) 3339-2727
¥¥¥

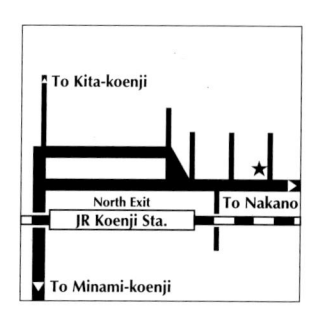

Dance and Prance

Dance clubs in Tokyo are bandits of the night. It is easy to get a license for liquor in Japan, but impossible to get a license for dancing after midnight. About 15 years ago, three teenage girls were picked up in a disco in Shinjuku after midnight and subsequently became the victims of rape and murder. By some inscrutable logic, dancing after midnight was therefore made illegal. For this reason many clubs will cite their closing time as midnight—even if they've just told you that they open at 11 p.m. If they openly flaunt their hours, then you'll know that they are paying the right people (and you'll be safe). Because of this law and the paranoia associated with it, the hours listed in this section may not match reality.

Whether legal or not, dance clubs are dependent on their DJs. They set the mood and create a following. Many boppers choose a club because a specific DJ is playing. Everybody is fussy about what will flick their switch and get them dancing, so many clubs feature different DJs on different nights to try and reach as wide an audience as possible. The fads and favorites never remain fixed for long. DJs come and go like the songs they play. Clubs that move with the market are always the freshest, but they are also the hardest to pin down. Small underground groups of kids sometimes set up a venue for a few months. They really hop for a while, then fly-by-night, but they're the coolest if you can find them.

Dance and Prance

Bland, prepackaged clubs have not been included. Take the excruciatingly boring Maharaja chain, for example. It will never change, so I can tell you exactly what you're not missing. You'll find snooty staff who behave like they're doing you a favor when they take your money at the door, lousy service even if you manage to get the bartender's attention, incredibly uninspired music, and unimaginative patrons who sway in front of mirrors and call it dancing. Even if you get VIP-room treatment, the atmosphere will be the same. These are the sort of clubs that hire *sakura*— a young couple whose job is to break the ice on the dance floor once guests start to arrive. No one wants to be first in this kind of bland clubland.

Another phenomenon which I have avoided is the menu approach to partying. The Nittaku Building in Roppongi has five floors of clubs all owned by the same company. When they entered the leisure industry they decided to hedge their bets and put a different genre club on each floor of the building. This vertical structuring runs oddly perpendicular to the idea of changing your DJs throughout the week. Each floor is a prepackaged party hell. Hitting a button in the elevator is like ordering from a vending machine. If you want disco, hit the B2 button. If you want 50s/60s, hit 2. If you want Latin, hit 3, etc. The aftertaste is as unappetizing as its fast-food equivalent.

The important thing is to plug in. The clubs I have omitted are easy to find—they advertise. The clubs I have listed will give you leads into Tokyo's real party core, so gear up and get ready for the meltdown.

The Deep

This is a fairly quirky venue in that it is only open on the weekend. During the week it is a gallery featuring exhibitions by up-and-coming local and foreign photographers. On the weekend, someone will occasionally organize an underground film festival of the Russ Myers/John Waters ilk. These tend to run in the early evening and then the club kicks in around ten or eleven p.m. By midnight the star DJs hit the turntables and a few seriously cool regulars start drifting in to dance. Although it appears in club listings, it is generally a very tight clique of partiers who come here to while away the morning. This is partly because it is very hard to find—but now you have a map. I will add a warning to this—it is *not* a pickup joint and it *is* a very tight, underground group of people who come here. So, unless you're as com-mitted to cool as the concrete that lines the walls in this place, you probably won't enjoy it. They serve imported beer in cans, including Grolsch.

Open from 11 p.m. till 5 a.m. every Friday and the 1st and 4th Saturday of the month. Suzuki Bldg. B1F, 8-12-15 Akasaka, Minato-ku. (03) 3796-0925 ¥¥

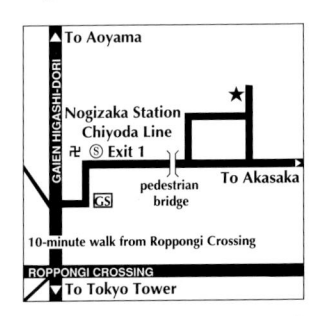

Dance and Prance

Cleo Palazzi

If you're a young African-American male who loves Japanese girls or if you're a cool white dude who knows his way around the ghetto, this is the club for you. They have the best local and foreign DJs spinning the funkiest rap and hip-hop you'll hear in this city. Men go to dance and party but they also go to pick up girls—so know the score or take a chaperone. The interior is completely black as are most of the clientele. There were only half a dozen white or Hispanic faces there last time I went, and even though I had a brother as an escort, he was asked (not me!) whether I was available. Loads of Japanese women (not girls) hang out here too—*yellow cabs* who've decided to save the fare to New York. It's a skanking scene and well worth it if you think you've got what it takes to cut it in this sort of clubland. If the bartenders are *genki*, they will break into a routine when their favorite vinyl hits the turntable. You can keep your eyes wide open and still not feel like you're in Tokyo.

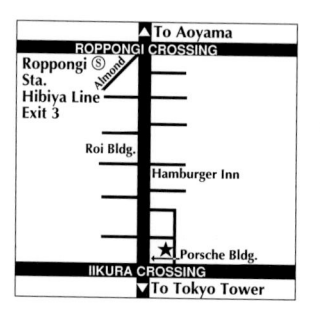

Open from 8 p.m. till 4 a.m. on Friday and Saturday only.
3-18-2 Roppongi B1F, Minato-ku.
(03) 3586-8494
¥¥¥

Dance and Prance

Eros

The only way to describe this place is as a total dive. The young and manic will find it extremely appealing, but unless you fall into this category I would advise that you give it a miss. It is dark, dingy, and covered with black-light graffiti. The walls are misshapen, evolving here and there into various seamy-smelling, cave-like grottos as they branch off the central dance floor. One of these nasty little caverns houses a large unadorned bed, which obviously inspired the club's "Lovenest" tag. This is Tokyo, however, and I have yet to witness or hear that it has been put to any use other than sitting. It gets totally packed on the weekend with the cream of Tokyo's wasted youth, who flock here to bop to machine-gun metered techno-house music. You would gain valuable cultural insights were you to conduct an anthropological study of Japan's *shinjinrui* on these premises. This is the kind of place that parents hate but kids count the days till they can go again.

Open from 8 p.m. till 12 a.m.
Sunday to Tuesday and on
Thursday, and till 5 a.m. on
Friday, Saturday, and
Wednesday.
Uchida Bldg. B1F,
4-12-6 Roppongi,
Minato-ku.
(03) 3404-5531
¥¥¥

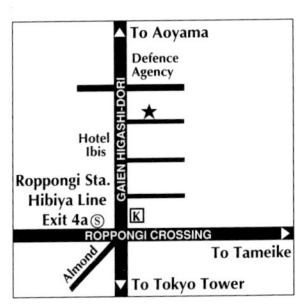

Dance and Prance

J Trip End Max

The J Trip conglomerate runs the hippest chain of clubs in this city and this one is their best. It is a very cool dance venue patronized by young, fun, and funky locals and a sprinkling of *gaijin* who have already infiltrated. It is also big. The second basement houses a large dance floor where you can bop till you drop—and that's what you'll want to do when the DJs are really cooking. The interior on this floor is suitably industrial with bare concrete walls and a small hideaway bar area at one end. Upstairs you will find a more subdued and comfortable atmosphere with low tables and couches where you can take a break from the frantic pace below. They play a lot of classic funk, soul, and rock on this floor, so you may not want to stop dancing if you go upstairs for a break. It does make a nice retreat from the blood-boiling thumpety-thump house music downstairs, though. This is one of the few clubs in Tokyo that almost achieves that dark, heady, and mysterious New York feel.

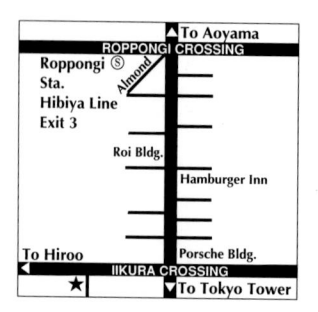

Open from 7 p.m. till 2 a.m. Sunday to Thursday and till 5 a.m. on Friday and Saturday. Hara Bldg B1F & B2F, 3-4-18 Higashi-azabu, Minato-ku. (03) 3586-0639 ¥¥¥

Java Jive

In my hall of fame for staying power, this venue rates an honorable mention. It is still going strong after the best part of a decade—in fact, it's predecesor in the same space managed an equally long stint. On the weekend, this large two-story basement venue attracts a faithful flow of expats, models, GIs, and some brave new local adventurers. Because of the club's no-rowdies-allowed door policy, it is a reasonably well-behaved group of partiers who end up thronging the dance floor and bar areas until closing. The walls are swathed in cute island-inspired graphics featuring repetitious silhouettes of dancing girls in grass skirts. A rough-hewn staircase connects the club's two interior floors, but its unevenness requires some negotiation after a few drinks. They used to have a novel sand-pit dance floor, but the band complained of sore throats so it was removed. Live reggae starts from eight p.m. with DJs dishing up an excellent mix of house and Latin dance favorites in between sets.

Open from 6 p.m. till 5 a.m. every day.
Square Bldg. B1F & B2F,
3-10-3 Roppongi,
Minato-ku.
(03) 3478-0087
¥¥¥

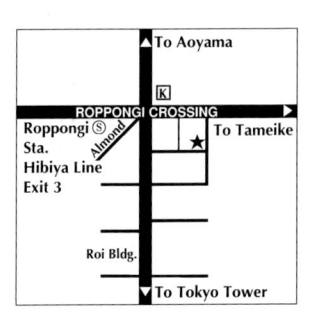

Dance and Prance

Cave

Unpredictability has been this venue's middle name since it opened a few years ago. Nothing ever stays the same, but the heaves and sighs of a changing clientele are almost audible in this club. The nuts and bolts of the place make going here worthwhile, so to avoid disappointment in terms of who else you might find, I suggest taking your own group of party people. Two sizable black-as-night dance floors and an excellent range of DJs throughout the week make dancing here a highly contagious and deliciously addictive activity. The darkness quotient also makes it a great place to brush up your steps if you are at all shy. One of the only drawbacks is the club's relatively small mezzanine bar area. Sweaty, dehydrated escapees from the dance floor practically line the length of the interior waiting for some relief. But, as the dance floors are so dark, this will be your only opportunity to check out who's there. Despite its variability, it remains a fairly hip place to hang out.

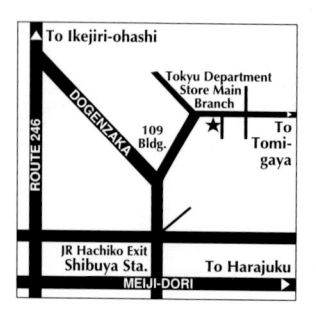

Open from 8 p.m. till 3 a.m. Sunday to Thursday and from 7 p.m. till 5 a.m. on Friday and Saturday.
M&I Bldg. B1F & B2F, 34-6 Udagawa-cho, Shibuya-ku.
(03) 3780-0715
¥¥

J Trip Bar Dance Factory

This venue offers a unique opportunity for firsthand observation of the *Shibu-kaji* (Shibuya casual) set— that mob of Japanese youngsters who dedicate their lives to the L.L. Bean catalog, but who think they are assuming a kind of Californian cool. This sociological offshoot from Tokyo's ever-evolving selfish youth have found (or rather created) their niche in this basement dance hall. Don't be fooled by the colorful psychedelic retro-60s murals all over the walls—you won't see too many punters who match the decor. The crowd depends on the night but they always tend toward young. Various DJs have regular slots on different nights of the week ranging in bias from soul to neo-surfer music—so check ahead to make sure. On the weekend, you can get down to a suitably mixed bag of hyper dance and disco. No bogus place this, dudes. There are not many dance clubs worth knowing about in Shibuya besides this one and Cave, so people pile in on the weekend.

Open from 6 p.m. till 12 a.m. Sunday to Thursday and later on Friday and Saturday. Kokusai Bldg. B1F & B2F, 3-16 Udagawa-cho, Shibuya-ku. (03) 3780-0639 ¥¥¥

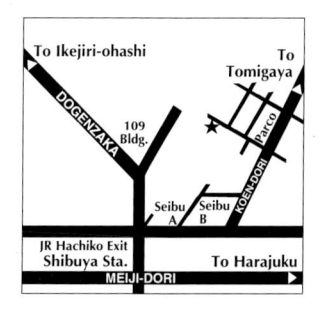

Dance and Prance

Juliana's

Wembley Japan, part of an international leisure specialist group, made sure they did their homework before opening their Tokyo club. The Japanese like a little pomp, splendor, and snob value when they step out in the evening. Appropriately aloof door people wearing snappy shoulder-padded jackets and wireless headsets control admittance. The entry is like the airlock in a spaceship. Tendrils of dry ice from the laser show inside enfold you as you enter the enormous belly of the beast beyond. A large central dance floor is flanked by ringside viewing and dancing platforms with adjacent bar and seating areas. Mezzanine VIP lounges are strategically located in see-and-be-seen corners. A host of international staff, including DJs and lively dancers, are employed by the club to pump up the vibe—and they do. The only drawback is the clientele. They tend to be a very average *Homat* and *salaryman/OL* mob, but maybe that's because it's so expensive. Don't forget your wallet.

Open from 6:30 p.m. till 12 a.m. every day.
1-13-10 Shiba-ura, Minato-ku.
(03) 5484-4000
¥¥¥¥¥

Dance and Prance

DJ Bar Ink Stick

In spite of the fact that this club is located on the top of a fairly modern building in Shibuya, it feels like a converted barn on somebody's lower forty. It is a big, dimly-lit, and sparsely furnished space with a bar down one side and a DJ booth in one corner. Whoever decorated the interior scores high marks for originality. The entire roof is hung with an interesting assortment of hats, like an upside-down mushroom farm, and the walls are variously covered with collections of hubcaps, wooden boot-sizers, and masks. I've put this venue in the Dance and Prance chapter because of its size and potential, but the average habitue tends to just sit and drink. Don't waste this dance space, Tokyo! It is plugged into the cool and groovy DJ circuit with all the familiar names appearing on the schedule. The music ranges from reggae to mod, which draws an impressive lineup of retro step-throughs out front. It's a little bit cool on an average night, but could definitely handle some heat.

Open from 6 p.m. till 2 a.m.
Sunday to Friday, and till 4 a.m.
on Saturday.
Campari Bldg. 4F,
1-6-8 Jinnan,
Shibuya-ku.
(03) 3496-0782
¥¥

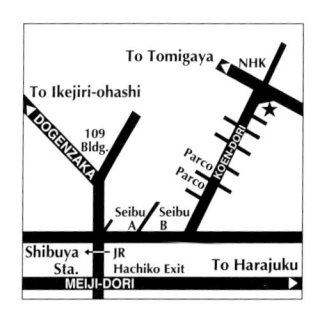

Dance and Prance

328

Nishi-azabu is becoming increasingly populated with bars, but this one has been here virtually unchanged for a decade. It's entrance, which has unexpected stairs and doors, is extremely hard to negotiate, so watch your step if you're a bit drunk or if it's your first time. Once through this initial obstacle course, you will find a large glassed-in room with an interestingly-shaped solid-wood bar running down its length. Beyond this is a DJ booth and dance area. They have made good use of some of their former record collection by plastering the walls with LPs—some of them are quite new, too. It is very quiet during the week and highly variable on the weekend, but it is best placed in this chapter because that's what they're aiming at. The DJs have a less stylized approach to their playlists, adding more rock and funk than other stuck-on-house clubs. They occasionally feature a soul night during the week, which makes it an excellent place for a late-night drink and a bop or a foot tap.

Open from 8 p.m. till 4 a.m. from Monday to Thursday, till 5 a.m. on Friday and Saturday, and till 3 a.m. on Sunday. Kotsu Anzen Center Bldg. B1F, 3-24-20 Nishi-azabu, Minato-ku. (03) 3401-4968 ¥¥

Dance and Prance

Yellow

The owners of a very popular late-night dance venue called Club Next decided to close down and reopen in a new and larger venue around the corner. This is Yellow. It's big, it's dark, and it's popular. The dance floor is spacious but quickly fills up, generating enough body heat to compete with high noon in mid-summer. A mezzanine bar and seating area overlooks the flesh-pit below, but when it's really crowded there is no escape from the heat. Lockers get scarce early and the coat check is usually full, so if you plan to get there late don't take a lot of gear with you. A few tragic teenagers camp in the stairwell waiting for the first train, but for the most part, it is a very hip and very cool cross section of Tokyo which comes here to dance till dawn. They feature excellent local and international DJs playing the latest house and dance hits from around the world, and also host a wide variety of events, including some live and gay nights. The best idea is to drop by and pick up a schedule.

Open from 9 p.m. till 5 a.m. or later every night. Sometimes closed on Sunday.
Cesaurus Bldg. B1F & B2F,
1-10-11 Nishi-azabu,
Minato-ku.
(03) 3479-0690
¥¥¥

Dance and Prance

Zoo

Though Shimo-kitazawa features very few dance clubs making Zoo the unchallenged winner, this venue would hold its own when compared to many Roppongi clubs. It has evolved as the headquarters of Tokyo's truly cool and very young up-and-coming clubbing crowd. This place has atmosphere, but not the sort of superficial attitudinizing you find in Tokyo's mega-clubs. It's an almost tangible and slightly brooding atmosphere that hangs in the air like the sulk on a teenager's face—desperate to be recognized but slightly unsure of asserting itself. These kids have definitely got potential. Foreigners are not uncommon, but they are mostly low-budget western-suburb ghettoites who are similarly young and living on the edge. You'll find no high rolling or high heels in this club. Some say Tuesday is best, some say Thursday, but just like a teenager's mood this can change on a dime. So go check it out, but if you're over 25 be prepared to feel like a grandparent.

Open from 8 p.m. till 4 a.m. every day. Open from 9 p.m. on live nights.
Central Bldg. B1F,
2-14-7 Kitazawa,
Setagaya-ku.
(03) 3413-2266/3413-2428
¥¥

Pickford Live Hall

This is definitely a dancing venue. Though the club itself is not very big its value is enormous if you prefer your music live. Two very polished bands take turns delivering cover versions of the latest hits from the dance charts with a few funky favorites thrown in for good measure. The lineup of performers includes Americans, Africans, Filipinos, and Japanese, but regardless of who is up on stage at any given point, you are sure to be entertained with very slick show-time renditions of some of your favorite dance tunes. It is well-run and reasonably well-appointed. The dance floor could be bigger, but here as with every-where else, this only seems to be a problem on the weekend. The price is a little steep for your average punter—¥3,000 at the door does not include drinks. So, if you have some fun-loving business pals in town on an expense account for a few days, they would not be disappointed with a night out here. Even if you treat yourself, it would be well worth every penny.

Open from 8 p.m. till 5 a.m. Monday to Saturday. Closed on Sunday.
Roppongi Raidick Bldg. B1F, 4-11-13 Roppongi, Minato-ku.
(03) 3423-1628
¥¥¥¥

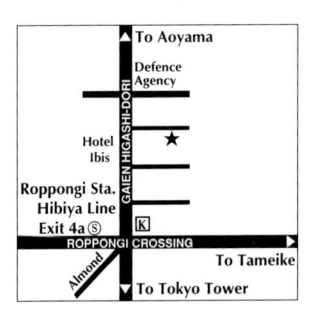

Dance and Prance

Ink Stick Suzue Factory

The original Ink Stick was a very small but very chic downstairs club near the Boecho. That venue has since become a flamenco bar but Ink Stick has moved on to bigger and better things. The Suzue Factory is a large, modern, well-designed split-level club featuring interesting local bands and a variety of overseas acts ranging from jazz through ska to hip-hop. Quality live music has always been a priority. The entrepreneurial insight of the management in the days of the original venue led to Sade's first break in Japan. The decor is refined and the lighting subdued. The first floor is set up for dancing and mingling while the mezzanine is furnished with tables and chairs overlooking the stage. Separate bars service each level. If you go on a live night, the crowd will vary according to the band both in terms of who goes and how many people. But, if you drop by midweek on a non-live night, you'll pretty much have the place to yourself. This is definitely one of Tokyo's more up-market venues.

Open from 6 p.m. till 11:30 p.m. every day, and till 4 a.m. on live and event nights.
Suzue Baydium Bldg. 1F & 2F,
1-15-1 Kaigan,
Minato-ku.
(03) 3434-1677
¥¥/¥¥¥

Buzz

This was the boppers' choice of disco when it first opened a couple of years ago. Lots of local Bobby Brown impersonators clad in baggy suits and Doc Martin's flocked here in droves. They pranced about in front of their favorite music videos like religious supplicants imitating the movements of their gods. The club manages to maintain a following because of its reasonably large dance floor and giant video screens. It is extremely young and crowded on the weekend, but sparse enough during the week to comfortably accommodate your mom and dad—this would be a safe choice were they interested in sampling some of Tokyo's nightlife. All the staff graduated from the same too-cool-to-fool school of catering from which Roppongi's prepackaged discos hire. They are efficient and attentive, if a little snooty—just the sort of treatment that impresses moms and dads, but who else? The floor is a little uneven in places (especially around the tables), so watch your feet.

Open from 6 p.m. till 5 a.m.
every day.
Square Bldg. 5F,
3-10-3 Roppongi,
Minato-ku.
(03) 3470-0088
¥¥¥

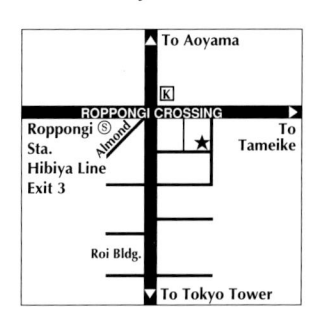

Ethno-bop

Ethnic was recently an over-used term in Japan. A few years ago it became the trendy word in advertising and marketing circles in Tokyo. It seemed that every new product was either named with a hybrid ethno-something word or draped in an ethno-something environment. The Japanese love packaging. They also love anything that comes in a complete cultural package. Whether this is American 60s rock'n'roll or a lesser-known tribe of Africa, it doesn't matter. As long as it has a defined lifestyle attached to it, the Japanese will find it fascinating.

The impact of these recent media campaigns was to generate a generic hype for anything ethnic. A trickle-down effect from this was a steady growth in the popularity of ethnic restaurants and bars. This was fairly across-the-board in terms of the variety of food that became available—everything from African couscous to Malaysian rendang. The most significant effect on Tokyo's nightlife was to endorse two of the city's longest running and most popular ethno-cultures—Latin and Rastafarian.

Japan's connection with Latin countries is long and well recorded. Beginning with the early Portuguese missionaries through to the recent bizzare popularity for Asian-eye operations among Peruvians seeking Japanese adoption, each culture continues to have a presence in the other. The annual Asakusa Samba Festival has become increasingly popular, attracting

Ethno-bop

more local samba schools to enter floats and dancers every year. This is an intriguing slice of carnival in the heart of old downtown Tokyo. Its existence is proof that opposites attract—a traditionally austere and conservative culture shedding its cool for the warmth and wildness of a feisty impulsive one. Before the recent upsurge, Latin clubs were either neighborhood cantinas or fancy little joints with a stage show. Now there's everything in between as well. If you want to find a party vibe, try a Latin bar.

Meanwhile, back on the isle, our brothers from the Antilles have found a niche on this isle, too. This is another textbook example of opposites attracting, but in this case it's the manic super-*salaryman* image of the modern Japanese that is being shed for the slow and steady hypnotic paradise of the Rastaman. The attraction for this flip-side lifestyle is understandable. Trading another appointment with your ulcer for a date with a palm tree, no matter how imaginary, has obvious appeal to some. Another plus is that you don't have to do anything to be a Rasta—don't cut or comb your hair, don't wear a suit, don't buy into Babylon, and, in this case, don't do anything illegal either. This is Japan. Many reggae devotees have developed their stance so well that they look as incriminating as Bob Marley on any of his record covers, anyway. The mood is very introverted in reggae bars. This is because the bass is usually up so loud that you feel the music more than hear it. People don't talk—they dance. It's a pretty cool-running scene, just sans the palm trees and herb garden.

Piga Piga

This has always been a happening place for people who like letting go to the earthy rhythms of live African music. The owner, himself part African-American and an accomplished musician, has been booking bands from the motherland since the club began. The interior looks more like a restaurant than a venue with a sea of tables and chairs crowding out the space, but people somehow manage to find room to dance. As with most establishments that import their entertainment, the minimum tenure is equivalent to a three-month entertainment visa, but regardless of who is playing, you will be guaranteed excellent quality. Tokyo's foreign community has enjoyed this venue and its vibe for years, and even the club's Japanese clientele seem to be transported to another world (once they've had a couple of drinks and the band cranks it up). It appears to have unlimited appeal by having cut across social and cultural barriers to attract a wide variety of partiers.

Open from 6 p.m. till 1 a.m.
Monday to Saturday. Closed on
Sunday and holidays.
Nanshin Ebisu Bldg. B2F,
1-8-16 Minami-ebisu,
Shibuya-ku.
(03) 3715-3431
¥¥¥

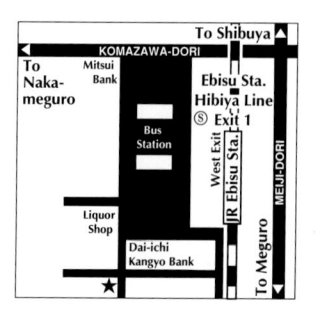

Bodeguita

During the week, this place operates as a colorful, if mild-mannered, Brazilian restaurant. On the weekend, however, Tokyo's Latino population turns up in force and in a dancing mood. Tables and chairs are pushed back as far as they will go and into the tiny vortex swarms a frenetic mass of bodies. Wall to wall people wriggle and wobble to salsa, samba, merengue—you name it (and the dancers usually can). Be prepared to rub up against a lot of bodies if you want to make it to the bar for a drink. This is authentic down-home partying, which should be avoided by claustrophobics or people who prefer to make reservations for a night out. Unattached women will be cavalierly asked to dance and politely thanked afterwards—if you avoid stepping on anyone's ego. Reminds you of another era, doesn't it? Japanese and gringo customers are scarce, so brush up your "hablas Español" and dust off those cha cha heels. It's cheaper than a ticket to Rio but definitely just as much fun.

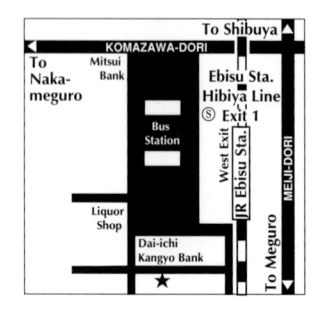

Open from 6 p.m. till 12 a.m. Monday to Saturday. Kitchen closes at 11:30 p.m. Closed on Sunday and holidays.
New Life Ebisu Bldg. 2F,
1-7-8 Ebisu,
Shibuya-ku.
(03) 3715-7721
¥

La Cabaña

When you spot this club from the street you expect to hear the music from a carrousel or the sounds of a carnival. It looks very festive and colorful, with giant perspex panels representing the flags of various Latin-American countries forming a plexi-tent exterior. Though a fairly recent addition to Tokyo's salsa circuit, it is the owner's second venture, though he unfortunately closed his Colombian hangout to keep this one going. When it first opened, the revelers from Bodeguita would pour through the door in sweaty droves eager to continue dancing the night away. The spacious interior allowed them to do so in more of a Spanish-Harlem block-party atmosphere. The result-ing high spirits and machismo inevitably led to fights, which were definitely discouraged—usually by closing early. To avoid this there is now a fairly steep minimum charge of ¥3,500 for hombres and ¥2,500 for chicitas. As most of the patrons were poor students, it is now usually empty and lacks the spark it once had.

Open from 6 p.m. till 12 p.m.
every day and till later on Friday
and Saturday.
Daikanyama Takara Bldg. 1F,
1-5-7 Kami-meguro,
Meguro-ku.
(03) 5721-3300
~~¥¥¥~~

Ethno-bop

Hi Time

Shinjuku is rife with reggae bars. They come in all flavors and offer varying degrees of dedication to Jah. This one is dark and throbbing and should appeal to serious devotees only. It is basically the after-hours equivalent of one of the area's best-known clubs—69. Everyone moves here en masse when that venue closes at midnight. If you miss the initial intake, you will have to wait at the end of a very long line to get in. Once inside, you will be treated to a powerful sound system delivering the sort of throbbing sense-o-round bass that really makes reggae work. As with many other establishments, however, the DJs do Japanese reggae-rap versions of Shabba Ranks et al, which can wear very thin if one is not pie-eyed enough. I wouldn't mind so much if they gave it a break once in a while, but once they start they just don't seem able to stop. In fact, they continue until their voices are so hoarse that it is actually quite painful to listen to. Take me back to the isle, mon.

Open from 9 p.m. till 5 a.m. every day.
Mano Bldg. B1F, 3-35-17 Shinjuku, Shinjuku-ku.
(03) 3357-4167
¥¥

Pigeon

When real dreads hit town, this is usually the bar that they settle into as a regular. I have asked them why and been told that the *master-san* delivers a more authentic Rasta vibration than any of his Japanese counterparts in other clubs. Even honkies seem to sense this authenticity. Gaz, who DJs at Gossips in London and plays with the ska band The Trojans, claims this as his favorite Tokyo bar. It is not hard to understand why. The interior is a little poky, and therefore extremely cozy, with a wooden floor and lots of potted plants. They play the best reggae in Tokyo—none of that painful ranking rapping and the DJ's playlist is not as trite as in other places. Also, two large monitors are well placed to pump you full of excellent videos of the same caliber. If you're hungry, you can tuck into a tasty Jamaican curry, too. It has been around for years and enjoys a loyal following, but it is not always crowded—maybe because it is a little expensive at ¥2,000 for your first drink.

Open from 8 p.m. till 3:30 a.m.
Monday to Thursday, and till
4:30 a.m. on Friday and
Saturday. Closed on Sunday.
Kokubo Bldg. 3F,
1-4-49 Nishi-azabu,
Minato-ku.
(03) 3403-2962
¥¥

Ethno-bop

AKA

Harajuku is a thriving hub of teen activity during the day, but by nightfall it has turned into a ghost town. One theory has it that this is in deference to its proximity to Meiji Shrine, one of Tokyo's most highly patronized religious institutions. The further away you get from the shrine, the more likely you are to find some nightlife. This tiny restaurant and bar is off Meiji-dori a block from Takeshita-dori. Even so, it closes at 12 a.m. You can drop by for a drink and listen to some cool-running reggae or sample some of their dishes made according to "recipes from old Jamaican grandmothers"—though these apparently include homemade pasta! They feature an interesting collection of beer from Trinidad (for connoisseurs of 50s-style beer bottles), Jamaica, Mexico (the mandatory Corona), and Brooklyn, N.Y. (would you believe!). The mood here is very low-profile, making it an excellent place from which to launch gently into the night (further away from the shrine).

Open from 12 p.m. till 2:30 p.m. for lunch and from 6 p.m. till 12 a.m. for dinner and drinks Monday to Saturday. Closed on Sunday and holidays.
Food Bldg. 1F,
2-18-8 Jingumae,
Shibuya-ku.
(03) 3478-3047
¥

Heartbeats

When I jump an express train out of Tokyo, I usually expect to leave the nightlife behind. A ride to the outer reaches of the Keio Line one night brought me to an unusual destination and a different conclusion—an out-of-the-way reggae bar with more character and appeal than many of its Tokyo counterparts. Ken-san, the owner, has been growing his dreadlocks and decorating his bar with curiosities from all over the world for well over a decade. The interior is large, but with bamboo stripping covering the walls and ceiling, candle light as the main source of illumination, and odds and ends tucked into and hanging from every conceivable nook and cranny, each corner has the intimate atmosphere of a cozy boudoir. Everyone from reggae devotees to relatively straight-looking *salarymen* and English teachers who live in the area drop by for a drink or a delicious curry. It is less than a two-minute walk from Keio Tamagawa Station and well worth the journey (even if you live in Chiba).

Open from 7 p.m. till 2 a.m. or
later every day.
5-7-6 Tamagawa,
Chofu-shi.
(0424) 86-9121

Cannabis Sativa

Black-light bars have become what the Japanese would call a *mini-komi* (minor market) trend over the past few years. Most of them combine surfing and reggae as common themes. This one is no exception, but the name has intrigued me—and many other people, I'm sure—for a long time. But no, you won't be greeted by a heavy dread rolling his eyes and offering you illicit substances at the door. In fact, it is a fairly well-furbished bar decorated in basic black with splashes of day-glo here and there to pick up the lighting. Also, it is run by very clean-cut bartenders who will definitely approach you, but only to take your drink order. Big picture windows offer excellent views of the poky little streets of Ueno far below. A row of monitors behind the bar show music videos. They only serve canned beers but feature an all-you-can-drink cocktail menu every night (¥1,500 for women and ¥3,500 for men). If you don't buy into this system you'll be hit up for a ¥500 cover charge.

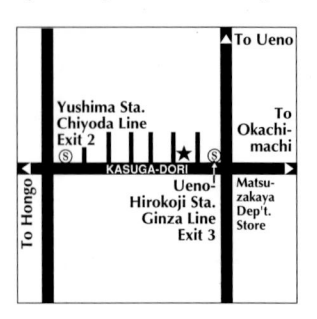

Open from 7 p.m. till 5 a.m. Monday to Saturday. Closed on Sunday.
Ueno 11 Bldg. 10F,
3-41-12 Yushima,
Bunkyo-ku.
(03) 3831-7777
¥/¥¥

> ## *Mix*

Omote-sando has a reputation for chic little boutiques and see-and-be-seen coffee shops, but not so much of a reputation for nightlife. This industrial-strength cement bunker tucked into the basement of a typical Aoyama office building, is about the only place that puts it on the map. Not only that, it is one of the most hauntingly real places that you will ever find in Tokyo. Nothing anywhere else comes even close to what you'll find here among its customers as a sense of commitment to the party edge. It is mostly patronized by hip young Japanese and a few of their older die-hard party counterparts, including the *master* and his friends. You will occasionally find a few starkly contrasting exceptions in the shape of expats who happen to live in the neighborhood and sometimes stumble in. It never fills up until well after midnight and does get crowded most nights of the week. The music is predominantly reggae except on Wednesday (bartenders' choice) and Thursday (house).

Open from 8 p.m. till 5 a.m. Monday to Saturday. Closed on Sunday.
Sanwa Jitsugyo Bldg. B1F, 3-6-19 Kita-aoyama, Minato-ku.
(03) 3797-1313
¥¥

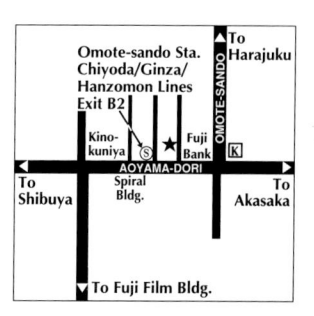

Sal Paradise

If you and a group of friends have just had dinner in Aoyama and everyone feels like grabbing a drink and maybe a dance afterwards, this would be a good place to take them. It's a little Latin-cum-reggae bar with a clean, smart interior painted in breezy graphics and adorned with a few potted palms. The *master* is Japanese as are his staff, who tend to be young reggae devotees. Because of this, you get an interesting mixture of up-tempo Latin rhythms and deep earth-moving reggae from the DJs. If there are enough people on the weekend, everybody gets down on the dance floor. Some punters will initiate group chorus lines of simple, repetitive dance steps to get everyone started. It depends on who's there. The clientele is an across-the-board mix of fairly straight office-working Japanese and English-teaching foreigners, but they and whoever else wanders in usually do so to party. If you're out on your own, there's definitely not much action midweek, but Saturday seems just right.

*Open from 9 p.m. till 2 a.m.
Monday to Saturday. Closed on
Sunday and holidays.
Katorea Bldg. B1F,
3-2-3 Minami-aoyama,
Minato-ku.
(03) 3403-4660
¥¥*

69

The most frustrating thing about partying in Tokyo is the synthetic quality of its clubs. You can almost hear the saran-wrap give as you enter most places. I mentioned this to some people I met just after I arrived and they took me here. In those days it really was something special—a dark and dingy gay reggae hole-in-the-ground with local dreads behind the bar and a cool but sullen-faced clientele. Why a gay reggae bar? Because it is in *the* gay part of Tokyo so a few of those brothers have always dropped by, and because the *master*, who looks exactly like Bob Marley, would occasionally jump up on the bar and strip down to his jock strap. He is busy running a reggae commune these days so he is hardly ever there. Also, the clientele has changed since it became popular with African exchange students. The interior is small and make-shift and there are no surprises on the DJs' playlist, but the place scores points for an unpretentious atmosphere and interesting mix of customers.

Open from 8:30 p.m. till 12 a.m.
every day.
Dai-ni Seiko Bldg. B1F,
2-18-5 Shinjuku,
Shinjuku-ku.
(03) 3341-6358
¥

Ethno-bop

Hot Co-Rocket

For years, this pleasant, spacious venue has been providing a stage for Tokyo's best live reggae. It is roughly divided by a step into two sections—an intimate bar area with booths and a high-ceilinged dance floor edged with tables. A new band, usually from Africa, takes up residence on the stage every three to six months. As with other clubs that change their band regularly, you will be guaranteed excellent quality no matter who's up on stage. In this venue, you will usually hear reggae-cum-love rock covers, with an original treat sometimes thrown in by the band. The lads are worked fairly hard, with 45-minute sets running from around eight p.m. until one a.m. every night. This club has always enjoyed a steady and enthusiastic audience, who are totally wound up by closing. The fairly steep cover charge, which only gives you two drinks, makes it less of a drop by club and more of an in-for-the-night spot. The Jah-vibration bar boys will ensure that you enjoy your stay.

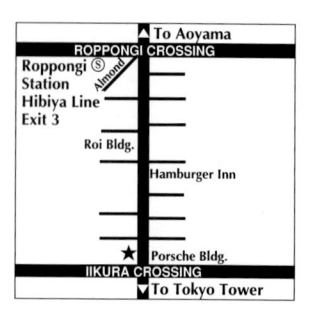

Open from 7 p.m. till 3 a.m. Monday to Saturday, and till 12 a.m. on Sunday.
Daisho #2 Bldg. B1F,
5-18-2 Roppongi,
Minato-ku.
(03) 3583-9409/3583-9424
¥¥¥

Saci Perere

You can count the number of clubs worth going to in Yotsuya on one hand. None of them are party places except this feisty little Brazilian nightclub, which in blinding contrast can get totally out of hand with drunkenness and revelry. Some nights it appears to be a well-mannered hostess club, the only ripple in the fabric of which is the occasional Latino girl flaunting the sort of décolletage a Japanese girl would die for. On other nights you'll wander headlong into a wild, impromptu samba line snaking recklessly through the club and in and out of back rooms. It is mainly expense account territory which attracts groups of corporate Japanese businessmen who sometimes have a foreign guest in tow. They feature excellent live Latin music every night, but the place really cooks when the owner's daughter gets the band jamming with her spine-stirring vocals. A little slice of carnival erupts on those nights. Hangers-on will be thrown out by one a.m.—the worst time to get a taxi in Yotsuya.

Open from 6 p.m. till 12 a.m.
Monday to Saturday. Closed on
Sunday and holidays.
P.L. Bldg. B1F,
Honshio-cho,
Kyuban-shi,
Shinjuku-ku.
(03) 3353-7521
¥¥

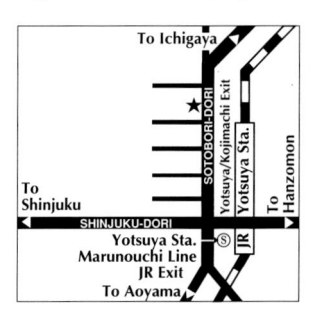

Ethno-bop

Jamaica Negril

The back streets of Takada-no-baba are beginning to spawn many interesting restaurants and bars as a result of the area's burgeoning student population. This reggae bar, which takes its name from a popular West Jamaican beach, is a welcome addition. The interior is neat, modern, and streamlined to accommodate a crowd—should one accidentally discover it. This hasn't happened yet, so you are likely to find it sorrowfully quiet on any night of the week. It is run by a resident Jamaican who employs some of his brothers behind the bar. The punters who drop by to drink are a very laid-back and friendly bunch who seem totally unperturbed by its emptiness. A trip to the bathroom is a real treat. You will find that the roof, walls, and floor have been covered in very cute marble-encrusted concrete. An interesting lineup of a dozen types of Jamaican rum are available, but the range of beers is very ordinary—Red Stripe is the only one in keeping with the owner's roots.

Open from 7 p.m. till 2 a.m. Monday to Thursday, and till 4 a.m. on Friday and Saturday. Closed on Sunday.
1-17-22 Takada-no-baba 1F, Shinjuku-ku.
(03) 3200-8864
¥

Salsa Corona

Tokyo has always boasted a variety of Latin bars, but recent years have seen an unprecedented boom. This one was all the rage when it first opened, but as with everywhere else, as soon as the spit dries out of the polish everyone moves on to the next newest thing. It is a decent size for sitting, drinking, or dancing, so there is plenty of room for them to add to their already firm (if small) set of regulars and survive the fickleness of Tokyo's barhoppers. The interior is warm and inviting with rough peach-colored plaster walls and rows of hand-painted tiles stripped in along the bar and other architectural details. If everyone who goes here does so on the same night, the result is a wild raging party with several couples trying to outdo each other on the dance floor. If you hit a slow night, you might have to knock back a few shots of tequila to get yourself and everyone else up and at it. It has great potential—but then, anywhere that makes an excellent margarita does in my opinion.

Open from 8 p.m. till 5 a.m.
every day.
Harrington Gardens Bldg. B1F,
7-7-4 Roppongi,
Minato-ku.
(03) 3746-0244
¥

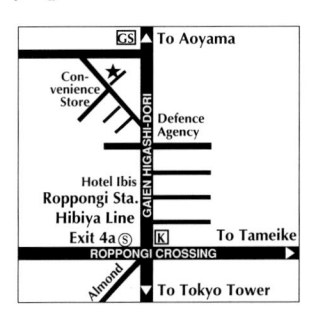

Ethno-bop

Kingston Club

One of the things I like most about Tokyo's reggae clubs is the predictable look of suspicion that the door and bar people level at non-regulars. They will even direct it at authentic Jamaican dreads, who have a lot of trouble figuring out just what is meant by this negative vibration. It is an inexplicable trait of this particular Tokyo scene and Kingston Club is no exception. What is most remarkable about this place is that it has survived for well over six years in a basement right in the heart of Ikebukuro's red-light district. Its location in part excuses the way strangers are greeted here. Inside, it is big and roomy and suitably dark, but the dance floor is slightly sunken— so watch your step. From eight p.m., the DJs start spinning some pretty cool tunes and only occasionally indulge in rap. Though the hours are listed below, they tend to close once the crowd thins out. Once you've broken the familiarity-barrier you may even rate a heartfelt smile at the door. Gee.

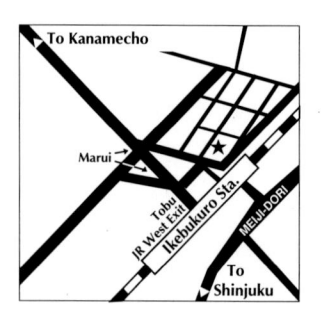

Open from 5 p.m. till 12 a.m. Sunday to Thursday, and till 2 a.m. on Friday and Saturday. Iwata Bldg. BlF, 1-24-4 Nishi Ikebukuro, Toshima-ku. (03) 3983-3719.
¥¥

Rum Bullion

If you haven't had enough good vibrations by the time Kingston Club packs it in, you might try staggering a few minutes further down the road to check out this little reggae bar. It has only been open for a short time, but relative to the ten barstools that it offers, it has already developed a loyal following among the insomniac residents of Ikebukuro. It has an incredibly high ceiling, which has been used to add a small mezzanine floor with cozy hideaway tables. If you sit at the bar, however, you will be surrounded by soft pink drapes hanging the full height of the interior. One row of these is set flush against the wall and a second row falls immediately behind the barstools, so that every seat and corner becomes enveloped in fabric. Tsutomu-san, who keeps things rolling until five a.m. every morning, is very young, very *genki*, and pleasantly flirtatious. He boasts some interestingly named and very sweet-sounding cocktails, which he says are aimed at his female customers.

Open from 8 p.m. till 5 a.m.
every day.
2-30-14 Nishi-ikebukuro 1F,
Toshima-ku.
(03) 5951-3455
¥

Club Jamaica

Talk about suspicious looks—this place takes the cake. In fact, if I hadn't been with an old club regular, I think I would have been thrown out for producing a camera. This is a word-of-mouth venue which has received some publicity in the past, but the owner actively discourages it. As long as you enter gently into a good night here you should have no problem. The *master-san* seems to know what he's doing as his club has already survived for years and probably will continue to do so—as long as no one blows too loud a whistle. The interior is a predictable patchwork of red, yellow, and green, and is appropriately indestructible and scruffy. Its truly distinctive feature is a solid 12-foot wall of stacked 15-inch woofers powerful enough to blow your toupee to Trinidad. No sign marks its entrance, but if you hold your breath for a moment on the pavement in front, you will feel its presence. Ask all your friends until you find one that knows this place and get them to take you along the first time.

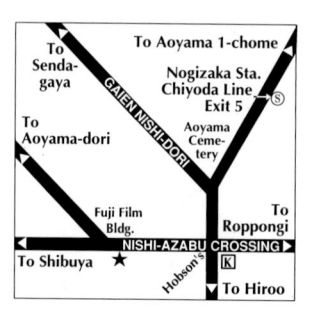

Open from 9 p.m. till 2:30 a.m. Monday to Thursday, and till 3 a.m. on Friday and Saturday. Closed on Sunday and holidays. Ishibashi Bldg. B1F, 4-16-4 Nishi-azabu, Minato-ku. (03) 3407-8844
¥¥

Acarajé

This bar would be just as much at home in Brazil as it is in Tokyo. Anji and Lisa, the Japanese-Brazilian couple who run the club, have created a down-home, Latin-style, neighborhood environment in which the city's overworked renegades can unwind. It has its wild party moments, when it is impossible to make it to the toilet without having to samba your way through. But it also has its soothing solitary moods, when a lone drinker might be the only customer holding up the bar. Everyone from Latino bar host-esses to stockbrokers seem to find this place appeal-ing. The Foosball table is well patronized, which ensures at least a few drop-bys every night, and the latest carnival videos play nonstop on a biggish screen. This club draws on three basic ingredients—Latin people, Latin music, and unpretentiousness. If you can't make a good start on the evening with these elements at your disposal, I suggest you spend your entertainment dollars on going to see a movie.

Open from 7 p.m. till 2 a.m.
every day, but often closed on
Sunday.
Emerodo Bldg. B1F,
1-8-19 Nishi-azabu,
Minato-ku.
(03) 3401-0973
¥

Gaijin Ghetto

Ghettos arise wherever there are clashes between classes or cultures. They are fueled by a non-assimilative attitude or a short-term approach. They are eliminated by economic and social osmosis—an interchange of goods or graces. If you have just hit town and know nothing of the culture or language, you will find yourself trapped in the Gaijin Ghetto.

Everyone parties differently. In the West we like to think we can handle our liquor. That is how we prove our party prowess—by either being able to keep up with the best or by drinking them under the table. In Japan, however, it is perfectly acceptable to act wildly drunk after just a few beers. In fact, at company parties it is almost expected. Because this idea runs counter to the Western party ethic, most foreigners find it unappealing. The clash between these party cultures spawned the Gaijin Ghetto and its bars.

Exposure triggers cultural osmosis. The longer you stay, the more you will want to move about the city. But unless you do your homework, you will be forced to communicate in English and limited to meeting those Japanese who speak it also. One in every ten of these encounters may end favorably, but mostly you will be relentlessly subjected to a standard set of questions haltingly delivered in your native tongue. Non-English speakers won't be safe either—a friend of mine used to pretend he was Polish until one local antagonizer turned out to be fluent in that language.

Gaijin Ghetto

Until you have broken this barrier, you will be forced to remain in the ghetto.

Osmosis is a two-way street. The Japanese who enter the ghetto are no longer playing by local rules. They are on different cultural turf—no structure, no format, no letting your coworkers pick up the mess. The cool Japanese who have lived abroad and whose conversational repertoire goes beyond the standard 20 questions, are hot on the Gaijin Ghetto trail. They want to maintain their hard-earned skill and, to some extent, show it off. In addition to these relatively sophisticated types are the hordes of local men and women who figure that a foreign partner would be an exotic and painless way of developing the same skill.

The ghetto is on the rise. More clubs open every year and many now employ foreign bartenders—customers who have jumped the bar to serve the Japanese. These *gaijin* barhops have in turn injected the scene with some of their own values—most notably, the tip. This is not normal practice in Japan, so to bring their attention to this ritual, a container is brightly labeled as the "tip jar" and placed squarely on the bar. It is sometimes rattled under your nose when you get your change, but its humble contents do beef up an otherwise miserable hourly wage.

You will be able to enter, order, and hang out in the bars listed here without ever having to speak Japanese. This will be invaluable for newcomers and a slice of home for old hands. So if you want to find a home boy or girl and a few smiling locals who are just dying to meet ya, drop by the ghetto.

Charleston

Charleston was a Tokyo institution. For many years it reigned unchallenged as the Gaijin Ghetto HQ in Roppongi, but this was mainly due to a lack of competition. It used to be the only no-cover-charge ghetto pit-stop before the influx of foreigners into Tokyo in the mid-80s. If you wanted a chance to huddle among fellow foreigners, this bar was pretty much it. The foreign influx created a mushrooming demand for such places and Charleston ultimately suffered a severe loss in clientele with the advent and proximity of its much more popular competitors, Dejavu and Gas Panic. These days there is not much reason to go there—unless you're into historical monuments. The taped music isn't very imaginative and (except for the cockroaches) it is usually empty. The upside of this is that you can enjoy a relatively unjostled drink on a Saturday night. No matter how many times it has been renovated, though, it still manages to seem dank and dingy.

*Open from 6 p.m. till 5 a.m.
every day.
Nakajima Bldg. 1F,
3-8-11 Roppongi,
Minato-ku.
(03) 3402-0372
¥*

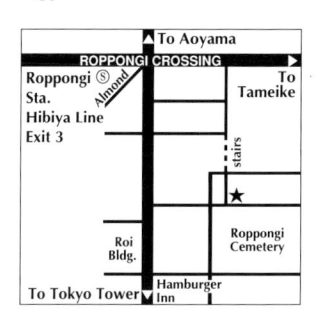

Gaijin Ghetto

Drug Store

This was the first 24-hour cafe and bar to open in Tokyo—a long overdue phenomenon for a city of this size. It has a slick, split-level modern interior with a bar on the main floor, comfortable seating and another bar on the mezzanine, and a refreshing outdoor area. You will also find a restaurant on the second floor and a personal-goods store in the basement. It used to attract a very laid-back and well-seasoned party clientele, who came to chat and linger until well after dawn. The nuts and bolts remain the same, but it now closes around five a.m. and has been taken over by yuppie desperadoes from hell. They flock here in droves after business dinners and proceed to unravel until closing. A few brave warriors from the party frontier drop by from time to time, but they mostly do so very late or end up congregating outside on the street. It is dead until ten p.m., but once the witching hour approaches, all manner of body snatchers pile in with that hungry for a take-away look in their eyes.

Open from 5 p.m. till 5 a.m. Sunday to Thursday, and till 7 a.m. on Friday and Saturday. The Wall 1F, 2F, & B1F, 4-2-4 Nishi-azabu, Minato-ku. (03) 3409-8222 ¥

Gas Panic

Welcome to a sinfully young and serious sleaze-pit. The interior shares the same *Star Wars* sort of decor as other bars of its type with an emphasis on concrete, graffiti, sawn-off mannequins suspended from the ceiling, and sticky floors from the inevitable spillage of drinks. A long bar leads you through the length of this mess and dumps you funnel-like into a small corral at the back surrounded by interesting arena-style seating. You almost expect a demented skinhead Nero to swagger in and declare, "Let the games begin!" The cheeky *gaijin* bar boys will hustle you for tips, but if you're not young, cute, and female you may find it hard to order a drink when it gets really crowded. The advantage of having this sort of bartender, though, is that they bring their own music, which is usually pretty fast and furious and delivered at decibels plus. When it gets completely packed on the weekend, the overflow of punters who are unable or unwilling to enter create a street scene in front.

Open from 7 p.m. till 5 a.m. Sunday to Thursday, and till 6 a.m. on Friday and Saturday. Shimojo Bldg. 1F, 3-14-8 Roppongi, Minato-ku. (03) 3405-0633 ¥

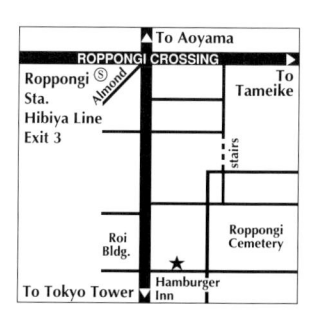

Gaijin Ghetto

Dejavu

This bar was the first, new-age era, no-cover-charge hangout to challenge Charleston's sultan of sleaze claim. It was every bit as grotty and bedraggled as all the other dives that have since sprung up, but it recently got a face lift which should last at least another week. People pour in on the weekend and tend to stay away during the week, making it a lot more tolerable on those nights. You will find the mandatory *gaijin* bar boys pumping drinks and the inevitable tip jar shoved in your face when you get your change. As it has been around longer than other bars of its kind, you will also find that it has a much more mixed bag of *okyakusan*. On any night you will find everyone from expats in business suits to sprout-eating new-agers to hungry-for-a-green-card Japanese. You'll also hear lots of twangy English as a second language and another grab bag of the bartenders' music. This is a rare educational opportunity to observe an Asian melting pot firsthand.

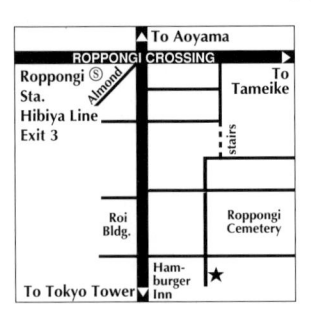

Open from 7 p.m. till 5 a.m. every day.
Togensha Bldg. #2 1F, 3-15-24 Roppongi, Minato-ku.
(03) 3403-8777
¥

Jirocho

Someone with a very fresh but slightly schizophrenic design sense outfitted the interior of this unique little hole in the wall. The facade downstairs doesn't promise much with its trite use of gnarly graffiti, but by the time you've reached its heavy wooden door you will have had your first taste of what's inside. The interior is outfitted with heavy wooden beams complete with finely painted, ornate carvings that have been recycled wholesale from an old temple. The floor is an uneven mosaic of cross sections from tree trunks. In addition to this spiritual and earthy look, however, they have added a very secular and Western element—swings. It is because of this curious feature that the bar is sometimes referred to as Swinging Chairs. They are taken out on the weekend so that more people can jam in—and they do—like commuters on the Yamanote at rush hour. It helps to be young to call this fun. The bartenders load up the cassette deck with an endless flow of reggae and rock classics.

Open from 8 p.m. till 2 a.m.
Monday to Saturday. Closed on
Sunday and holidays.
Sato Bldg. 2F,
2-8-7 Nishi-ebisu,
Shibuya-ku.
(03) 3477-2600
¥

Club Gas Panic

The owners of Gas Panic used to run a dark throbbing den for hooked-on-house junkies from these premises. Then they wised-up and restyled in the *gaijin* bar vein to accommodate their burgeoning clientele from their other bar. This one is referred to colloquially as Gas Panic 2 and it looks pretty slick right now. Judging by the parent bar, though, it should only be a few months before it takes on the aura of a dive in its own right. The interior is relatively spacious with a central bar and seating off to one side. The punters who are already mobbing the place are young and into nihilistic fun. Anyone you see on the street on an average night in Roppongi is likely to wash up here at some point. The *gaijin* bar staff are representative of some of Tokyo's more seasoned party boys and the entire bar is made of stainless steel just in case anyone wants to jump up and dance. It was already on the map as a pit stop before the restyling, so it should continue to be hot. At least this one has a toilet.

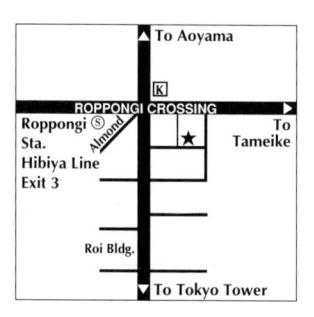

Open from 7:30 p.m. till 5 a.m. Monday to Thursday and till 7 a.m. on Friday and Saturday. Marina Bldg. 3F, 3-10-5 Roppongi, Minato-ku. (03) 3402-7054 ¥

Sunset Strip

If you are fed up with being shoved sardine-style into grotty little bars just to be with other *gaijin*, you might try this one next time. It is more up-market than other ghetto pit stops with a clean, modern interior that is still reasonably well-preserved after several years of operation. It features a full and well-stocked bar—you can almost call the label on any drink—and they keep my favorite local beer, Sapporo, on tap. The staff is extremely friendly and the overall atmosphere is very relaxed. It can sometimes explode into an anything goes party on the weekend, but don't expect a crowd midweek—even though drinks are half-price between seven p.m. and nine p.m. every day. You can take advantage of its relative emptiness if you have a large group in tow. MTV junkies will enjoy pumping coins into the jukebox to see their favorite videos, but the bartenders sometimes ban the most popular ones if they've already ODed—an occupational hazzard. Ah, but what else after a hard day's arbitraging?

Open from 7 p.m. till 5 a.m. Monday to Saturday, and till 2 a.m. on Sunday.
1-8-4 Nishi-azabu 1F, Minato-ku.
(03) 3404-9988
¥

Gaijin Ghetto

The Library

You would have to be more than just a bit desperate to include this very neighborhoody establishment on a night tour of Tokyo. It functions as an amenable enough bar for local residents, but its most valuable aspect for those of us who live further afield is that it also functions as a library. The owner, G. David Munoz (the G is for God from a father with a wicked sense of humor, so he says), prefers simply to exchange books these days rather than buy them outright. It is probably no bigger than ten mats with a bar area at the entrance and book-lined walls surrounding a seating area beyond. Business is not exactly what you'd call booming, but it has managed to maintain a loyal following among Tokyo's English-teaching fraternities. As usual, the weekend draws in the maximum crowd, who definitely get down and rowdy until very late. On other nights, a very laid-back and down-to-earth atmosphere pervades the place. Buritos and tacos are available on the weekend.

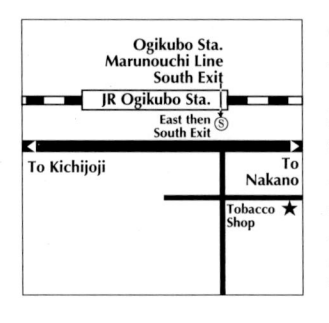

Open from 3 p.m. till 12 a.m. Saturday to Monday and on Wednesday, and from 5 p.m. till 12 a.m. on Thursday and Friday. Closed on Tuesday. Inadaya Bldg. 3F, 5-29-11 Ogikubo, Suginami-ku. (03) 3391-2164 ¥

Inaoiza

In terms of a hitchhiker's guide to the galaxy of Tokyo's nightlife, I would dub this my bar at the end of the universe. Though I can afford to be an inner-city snob, this is not so much a geographical place-ment as it is a psychological one. It has a mysterious frontier-pub sort of atmosphere that comes when a transient clientele derives a desperate comfort from the knowledge that they have reached the last outpost for miles. It is full of would-be space pirates, who must console themselves with still being on the hippie trail as we approach the 21st century, and anyone who can't afford or doesn't want to make it into town on the weekend. In fact, most drinkers here seem to take an almost perverse delight in having snubbed Tokyo's more obvious party meccas for the night. They can feel completely justified as this place has an authentic cool in a warm, settled environment. Some interesting local bands play here for a nominal music charge. You can also grab a tasty bite to eat.

*Open from 7 p.m. till 2 a.m.
Wednesday to Monday. Closed
on Tuesday and holidays.
Sunny Mansion Bldg. 2F,
2-38-16 Kita-koenji,
Suginami-ku.
(03) 3336-4480
¥/¥¥*

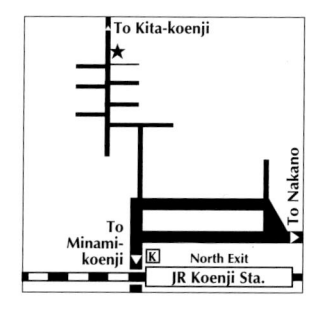

Gaijin Ghetto

Oh! God

If you arrived in Tokyo with a backpack instead of an expat package, this nightspot will prove to be very good value. It is a large, comfortable cafe and bar which serves as a local hangout for many new and old residents alike. There are two pool tables just inside the entrance which are equally well-patronized by foreigners and Japanese. The main room beyond houses a bar and counter in one corner and tables and chairs fill out the rest of its extravagantly-sized dimensions. The good value aspect of this place is that you can watch foreign feature films without any additional charge on the price of your drinks. Sometimes the sound is turned down, so unless you can read the Japanese subtitles or get one of the waiters to turn it up for you, this can almost be a tease. The overall atmosphere is very casual and laid-back. Most people just come to hang out and no one is in a hurry. A monthly schedule of movies to be shown is available at the door. The last run starts at three a.m.

Open from 6 p.m. till 6 a.m. every day.
Jingubashi Bldg. B1F,
6-7-18 Jingumae,
Shibuya-ku.
(03) 3406-3206
¥

Gaijin Zone

In recent years, Roppongi has spawned an endless array of bars aimed at catering to Tokyo's *gaijin* population. None of these bars has proclaimed it as obviously as this one has by its choice of name. True to the tradition that Dejavu started, you will find the *gaijin* bar boys, the tip jar on the counter, the black bouncer at the door, and a wild and woolly bunch of party animals eager to make good use of the bar and dance floor. Ghetto pit stops are, almost without exception, dirty and dingy like this one, but the management has at least spent some money on creating a Koh Samui-style thatched-roof and palm-tree interior. It is remarkably party-proof, as well. When it first opened it was *the* place for a while, but now it only seems to get crowded once all the other bars are full. One of the staff plays DJ on the weekend and usually manages to get the party vibe up and skanking. The upside of this club's fall from favor is that you may even have a little room to dance.

Open from 9 p.m. till 6 a.m. Tuesday to Thursday and on Sunday, and from 8 p.m. till 6 a.m. on Friday and Saturday. Closed on Monday.
3-8-6 Roppongi B1F, Minato-ku.
(03) 5410-6351
¥

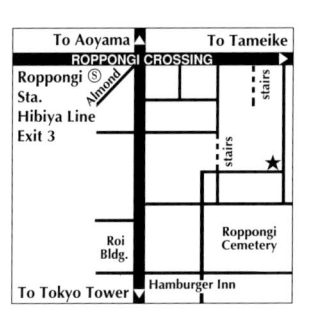

Gaijin Ghetto

Motown House

During the week, this is not such a bad place to slip into for a quiet drink with a buddy or two. You will probably get a seat and nobody will bother you unless you look like you want to be bothered. On the weekend, though, it functions as a meat market which is overly popular with *Animal House*-type fraternity boys and sorority girls. It gets packed! These punters are not exactly what the butcher would call choice cuts once they have been drinking at their usual gallon-a-second rate and they start singing along at the top of their lungs to such favorites as "Stand By Me." The presence of such songs on the playlist and the odd framed gold record by some better-known Motown artists are the only elements of the whole scene that give you any hint as to why the owners chose its name. The staff is actually very friendly when they're not being harrassed by the weekend hordes. So unless you like a little wall of flesh with your wall of sound, stick to midweek and avoid it on the weekend.

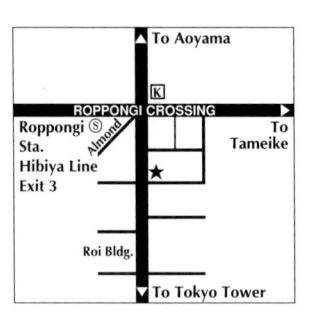

Open from 6 p.m. till 5 a.m. every day.
Com-Roppongi Bldg. 2F, 3-11-5 Roppongi, Minato-ku.
(03) 5474-4605
¥

Cafe Mogambo

Very few bars have a settled feeling when they first open, but this one did from the outset. Its rather modest size has been well used by placing an oval-shaped bar in the middle to service its 20 bar stools, and by lining the walls with pub-style stand-and-lean counters. On any night of the week, you'll find a few regulars already tucked into their favorite spots waiting for a friend or just killing time and curious to see who drops in. On the weekend, you'll find the same thing, except that it will be small groups of regulars either settling in for the evening or waiting for a tardy mate before they head off for more serious partying elsewhere. They employ *gaijin* bar boys, but they don't have a tip jar or an attitude. Some fairly average mementos from the owner's travels through Asia hang on the walls, but these meld pleasantly enough with other bamboo and earthy touches to create an unobtrusive drinking environment. It is a very adult and unfussy place for a quiet sanity break.

Open from 6 p.m. till 5 a.m.
Monday to Saturday. Closed on
Sunday.
Osawa Bldg. 1F,
6-1-7 Roppongi,
Minato-ku.
(03) 3403-4833
¥

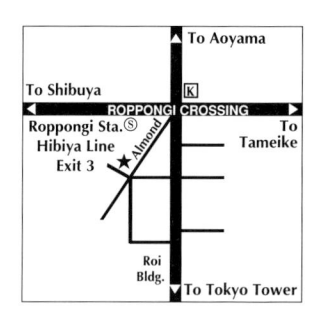

Cafe Presto

There is not a lot happening on the Seibu/Parco side of Ikebukuro Station, so this bar has quickly become the local for everyone in the area. It occupies two floors of a modern building which is a convenient two-minute walk from the east exit of the station. Over time, its two floors have developed two very different followings—a *gaijin* bar crowd downstairs and a Japanese coffee shop clientele upstairs. It is pretty laid-back midweek, but on the weekend the difference in atmosphere between the two floors is almost schizophrenic. Downstairs gets really packed with a fairly drunken cross section of work-a-day foreigners (including many Pakistanis these days). If you pop upstairs, though, you will find a very sub-dued group of Japanese quietly chatting over coffee. There is a laser juke box downstairs which, at ¥100 a throw, is an excellent way to familiarize yourself with the latest in Japanese music videos. You can also choose from a limited selection of foreign favorites.

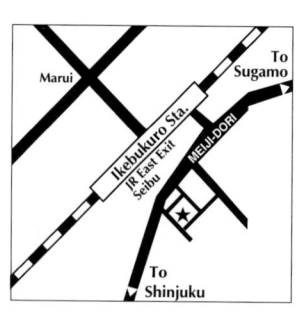

Open from 11 a.m. till 12 a.m. (1F) and till 11 p.m. (2F) Monday to Saturday, and till 11 p.m. on Sunday (both floors). Fuji Bldg. 1F & 2F, 1-23-1 Minami-ikebukuro, Toshima-ku. (03) 3971-2873 ¥

Pip's (Ya Ya Pub)

It is hard to believe that this subterranean den was once *the* swank hangout for Tokyo's arty party people 20 years ago. It then became *the* place for the seedy leftovers from other bars to wait for the first train home, but there are now many establishments vying for that honor. These days it is most notable for its giant pineapple facade and its sometimes extremely down-market clientele. This is especially true when hostesses start knocking off work and when the marines are in town, which is usually every Saturday night. It is hard to tell just what kind of scene you'll find, so I would strongly advise that you take your own (or wear a trenchcoat and sit in a corner). Every other time I drop by it actually seems rather dignified—lights down low, the warm glow of pinball machines, people huddled in conversation at tables, rock videos playing on a biggish screen. The next time it's like a zoo. One thing is fairly certain though—it is always empty until well after midnight.

Open from 5 p.m. till 5 a.m. every day.
Shuwa Bldg. B1F,
3-14-12 Roppongi,
Minato-ku.
(03) 3470-0857
¥

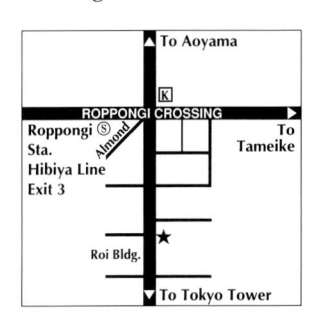

One Lucky

It is impossible for me not to feel nostalgic about this little neighborhood bar originally spawned by its proximity to the Kimi Ryokan. When I first came to Tokyo, the Kimi is where I stayed and this is where I used to drink. When the old Kimi was torn down a few years ago and a modern concrete version erected, One Lucky moved. The *gaijin* who stay at Kimi must now stagger further to reach it, but one thing that hasn't changed is its atmosphere. You will still find an interesting mix of new arrivals and old-timers, who'd follow the *master* to the ends of the earth, snuggled in at the tables knocking back drinks like there's no tomorrow. You must be a friend of the *master* to get in, as he thinks of it more as a members' bar. If you manage to leap this hurdle you may become accepted into his honorary family, which will inevitably lead to having your photo taken for the One Lucky hall of fame. Reaching this stage will give you entry to a great place for a chat and a serious bout of drinking.

Open from 6 p.m. till 2 a.m. (or earlier if it's slow) Monday to Saturday. Closed on Sunday and holidays.
3-33-5 Ikebukuro 1F, Toshima-ku.
(03) 3985-0069
¥

Henry Africa's

This was the first branch in what has become a chain of restaurants and bars, though nobody really comes here to eat. Its main function is as a bar, but it continues to drift in and out of favor with the expat drinking contingent. The advent of places like Dejavu and Gas Panic cut it short for a while, but it is currently back on the map. It attracts a very relaxed and jolly English pub crowd, but like anywhere in Tokyo, you can never tell just who might wander in. People come to drink and chat, watch music videos, and play Foosball soccer for ¥100 a throw. Perhaps the most remarkable aspect of this bar is that people don't mind doing all of these things in lighting that allows them to see who's sitting on the other side of the room. In spite of this, it has a very homey and lived-in feel. Japanese beer is half price between six p.m. and nine p.m. from Sunday to Thursday, when you can also help yourself to free plates of chicken, chips, and pizza. They also offer some reasonable deals for parties.

Open from 6 p.m. till 2 a.m.
Monday to Thursday, till 4 a.m.
on Friday and Saturday, and till
11:30 p.m. on Sunday.
Hanatsubaki Bldg. 2F,
3-15-23 Roppongi,
Minato-ku.
(03) 3403-9751
¥

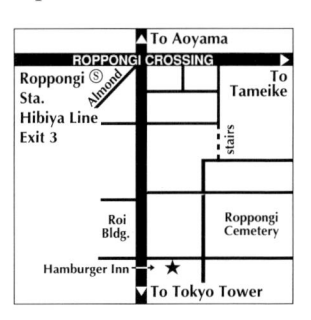

Gaijin Ghetto

Gasoline Alley

For many years, this has been an institution among Shimo-kitazawa's seedier dives. It recently underwent a face-lift so you've missed it at its worst. The owners trashed all the paraphernalia that once covered the walls and a lot of their old albums (which would have been a good night for the *gomi*). They then uniformly doused everything in bucket-loads of the same turquoise-green paint—the tables, the chairs, the walls, and even the gaffer's-tape repairs to the walls that speak of brawls gone by and alcohol-induced bouts of vertigo. A gold Grecian bust and some very real, omnipresent rats and cockroaches are the only decorations that remain from its former incarnation. When I got there at two a.m., there was a lone male *gaijin* drinker holding up the bar. "This is a place for guys to come and meet their mates and drink. Girls don't come here," he said. But actually, it seems like no one goes there anymore. Maybe they're waiting for the same old familiar smells to settle back in, too.

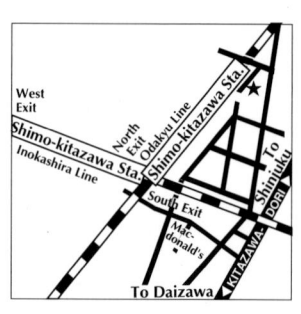

Open from 7 p.m. till 3 a.m. Monday to Friday, and till 5 a.m. on Saturday. Closed on Sunday.
2-9-17 Kitazawa, Setagaya-ku.
(03) 3460-5990
¥

Mother's Ruin

This is the new, sister establishment of Rock Mother, which is another Shimo-kitazawa institution but a clean and well-furbished one. Unlike my guess that Chizuko-san, the Rock-mama herself, was worried that opening another bar would send her broke, she chose the name for two other reasons: It's a euphemism for gin and the interior is fashioned to look like a ruin. The plaster walls are faced in broken brickwork and rough-blown glass. The length of the roof is home to an enormous copper lizard which looms dramatically overhead and cleverly conceals ventilation pipes with its tail. Lizards *do* bask in the sun of ruins, right—remember J.G. Ballard's *The Drowned World*? Great slabs of trees serve as tables and smaller ones as seats. In the only-in-Tokyo tradition, the bathroom has also been decked out in keeping with the interior theme. Drinks are a little more expensive here than at Rock Mother, so there may have been an element of truth in my hunch for the naming after all.

Open from 5 p.m. till 2 a.m.
from Monday to Saturday.
Closed on Sunday.
NF Bldg. B1F,
2-2-7 Kitazawa,
Setagaya-ku.
(03) 3412-5318
¥/¥¥

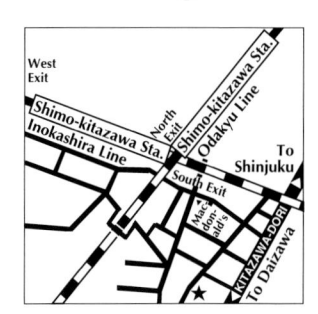

Rock Mother

Does anyone know or remember the British TV series "Dr. Who" that featured the spaceship *Tardis*? From the outside, it looked like an ordinary London telephone box, but through dimensional trickery, once you entered it was enormous. Similarly, the entrance to Rock Mother is deceptively narrow. It looks like a little log cabin with picture-book windows overlooking a small seating area, like that of a tiny coffee shop. Once inside, though, it seems to go on forever. The narrowness of the entrance creates an inconvenient bottle-neck along the length of the bar, especially when it gets crowded on the weekend. You have to push you way through to get to the seating area at the back, which also usually gets crowded. It is every bit as warm and toasty as the facade suggests, and attracts a robust throng of hearty drinkers whose numbers indicate that this is *the* neighborhood hangout of choice. It is also one of the cheapest places to drink in Shimo-kitazawa.

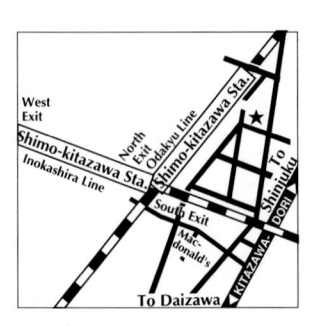

Open from 5 p.m. till 3 a.m. Monday to Saturday, and till 2 a.m. on Sunday.
2-9-22 Kitazawa, Setagaya-ku.
(03) 3460-1479
¥

New Sazae

Even compared to Roppongi's dives, this place is over-the-top sleaze for Tokyo. As the name suggests, there used to be an old Sazae, but the new one has been in the same spot for well over a decade. In fact, I've only met one person who ever went to the old one and that was in the 60s when he was here to perform in the musical *Hair*. The decor, if you could call it that, has never changed though occasionally they will repaint the walls and let the graffiti start from scratch. You are more than welcome to add your name to this ever-changing wallpaper. Heavily curtained windows make sure that no light ever enters these murky depths. This part of Shinjuku is *the* gay area of Tokyo so, although this is not a boys bar, you will find an interesting mix of customers—the odd transvestite in a frock, hard-nosed bleached-blonds from the suburbs, die-hard party animals, and sullen-faced voyeurs. All who enter lose a night in their life (and most of the next day).

Open from 10 p.m. till 5 a.m.
Sunday to Thursday, and till 6
a.m. on Friday and Saturday.
Ishikawa Bldg. 2F,
2-18-5 Shinjuku,
Shinjuku-ku.
(03) 3354-1745
¥

Gaijin Ghetto

The Rising Sun

Jerry Hegarty is the proprietor of this home-away-from-home for some of Tokyo's British-bent population. He started out by teaching English to save the money to open his own bar. He succeeded nearly 20 years ago and hasn't looked back. His cozy little establishment always has a steady flow of Japanese and expat patrons who come to knock back a pint or two and inevitably end up discussing rugby. Jerry is actively involved in organizing and refereeing local matches. Its proximity to a well-known aikido gym brings a few of those lads in as well. The decor is warm and woody with various Olde Worlde paintings and horsey paraphernalia hanging amid rugby team shots and the odd row of pewter mugs, which some customers bring and leave for their exclusive use. Jerry also offers a limited but tasty menu of home-made sausages and shepherd's pie. All this place needs is a dart board (and a little more space) to be considered an authentic English pub.

Open from 6 p.m. till 12 a.m. Monday to Saturday. Closed on Sunday and holidays. Shinsei Bldg. 2F, 1-9-3 Yotsuya, Shinjuku-ku. (03) 3353-8842 ¥

Crocodile

Every big city eventually evolves a headquarters for its renegade edge of musicians. If you have just arrived in Tokyo and find the nightlife a little too prepackaged and sterile, you might check this place out. It is a unique old establishment that has always provided a stage for the fledgling and leading edge of non-manufactured live music. Because a lot of the bands who play here are just starting out, I would not promise that they are all worth seeing, but they will definitely be aiming at something more interesting than the standard Japanese pop that you see on TV. The interior is quite spacious but quickly fills up on live nights. On a non-live night, however, you might try dropping by for a beer and a game of pool. It has been around for years, so it has a very settled and comfortable, if slightly idiosyncratic, atmosphere. Bands and cover charges vary depending on the act, as does the crowd, but overall it is a no fuss and genuinely down-to-earth establishment.

*Open from 6 p.m. till 2 a.m.
every day.
New Sekiguchi Bldg. B1F,
6-18-8 Jingumae,
Shibuya-ku.
(03) 3499-5205
¥/¥¥*

Les Girls and Boys

Tokyo's gay scene is vast but very closeted. An intricate web of discretion and secrecy interconnects and shrouds every facet to keep it that way. While Shinjuku 2-chome has the highest concentration of gay bars in Tokyo, you will find that most of their doors are kept firmly shut to newcomers. Even Japanese men will occasionally find it necessary to have an introduction from one of the club's regulars. This is especially true of S&M and specialist bars. It's a catch 22 situation—you can't get in to meet the people you need to know to get in.

Until recently, the scene was virtually unmapped. You can now buy a *Pia*-type guide in gay bookstores called *Otoko Machi Map*. Browsing through a copy will give you an idea of the number of bars, health clubs, massage parlors, shops, and video stores that cater to this market, and also an idea of the diversity of specialities among them. Another important point will also become apparent—*gaijin* are not always welcome. So a newly-arrived foreigner is at a double disadvantage with these ground rules.

The bulk of Tokyo's gay bars are typically Japanese. As one of my friends noted, they are a "mirror of the straight world"—except that the staff and patrons are exclusively men. Besides the ambiance factor, many Japanese gays are married and work in an office with women, so this is the last place they would like to be seen by a wife or coworker. In these bars, you will be

Les Girls and Boys

greeted with an *oshibori*, served a traditional *otsumami*, and chatted to amiably while your drinks are being administered. Unless you speak Japanese, you will be at another disadvantage. Newcomers to the scene consequently end up at a handful of establishments that function like Western bars, where English is spoken, and where *gaijin* are welcome. In these bars (all of which are listed) it will be easy to meet people and develop contacts.

There are also two gay beats for men. The first is Naka-dori in 2-chome. Everybody cruises the strip at some point in the night, even if they're only moving on to the next bar. This will give you a good idea of who's out partying. Also, anyone hanging around (especially in the bookshop) is usually doing so to meet someone. The other beat is in Komazawa Park behind the bleachers at night, but this is a no-questions, no-names situation for the brave only.

Tokyo's lesbian scene is tiny by comparison. I know of only four bars in Skinjuku 2-chome and one of those is usually shut. The other three are all on the same block and always seem to be empty. Because the scene is so small and men are not allowed, a fairly hefty cover charge is usually added to your bill so that the *mama-san* can make ends meet. It is a pity because I think it also keeps some women away. The good news is that foreign women are welcome. If you are a fun-loving lesbian, however, keep your eyes open for gay women nights at some of the hipper dance clubs. These are rare and have no schedule, but if you track one down you will be able to make better connections.

Les Girls and Boys

GB

Since Keiji, the *master-san*, reopened his club a few years ago, it has become *the* most popular meat market in 2-chome. Foreigners are welcome and will find Keiji's fluent English and friendly manner an invaluable asset for getting to know the scene. I did sneek a peek in the door one night and witnessed what I had been told that I would. The place was completely packed, making it difficult to see anything beyond a central bar completely surrounded by wall-to-wall flesh. All eyes faced each other—until they spotted me and I was gently asked to leave. This is not a butch bar. The customers are mostly young Japanese boys who come to flirt with expats. It is great for foreigners who've just hit town because nearly everybody speaks English, they play excellent music videos, and it has a good, anonymous singles bar atmosphere. It's a bit of a cliche for residents, but some do drop by just to see Keiji. It gets packed on the weekend with seriously intent Japanese and *gaijin*.

Open from 8 p.m. till 2 a.m. Monday to Thursday, till 2:30 a.m. on Friday, till 3 a.m. on Saturday, and till 1:30 a.m. on Sunday.
Business Hotel T Bldg. B1F, 2-12-3 Shinjuku, Shinjuku-ku.
(03) 3352-8972
¥

Les Girls and Boys

Kinsmen

Few bars in Tokyo can provide the kind of sophistication and intimacy that this little bar has to offer. It is also the only club in 2-chome that is truly mixed, both in terms of gay and straight and Japanese and *gaijin*. Its warm and tasteful interior was lovingly put together by Junji and Tomo, the cherubic couple who own and run the bar. An enormous earthy *ikebana* towers over the center of the club. It is skillfully crafted every week from branches of whatever's seasonal and, as it is so big and the space is so small, it practically fills the club. It has become such a trademark that people will always remember this detail no matter how hazy their memory is of the night before. Evenings midweek are generally very relaxed and casual, but the weekend sees the usual surge in numbers and, when GB is closed, the crowds can become unbearable. On some special nights, though, when there's something in the air and the choreographers are in town, the atmosphere is almost electric.

Open from 9 p.m. till 5 a.m. every day. Sometimes closed for a month during summer. 2-18-5 Shinjuku 2F, Shinjuku-ku. (03) 3354-4949 ¥

Mars Bar

As if to settle the door-policy score in the area, this club will only admit women. Because of this rule, however, you will nearly always find it empty—even though it only seats about ten. Being fully aware that she is serving a very small market, the *mama-san* tries to make economic ends meet by hitting her customers with an exorbitant ¥3,000 cover charge. This only entitles you to a small snack and does not include your first drink, which often sends even committed lesbians running for the nearest straight bar. It is very pleasant, however, and is obviously providing its regulars with a necessary outlet, as this is the longest running club of its kind in the area. The atmosphere is very low profile and discrete, with women pretty much keeping to their own groups, though the odd *Takarazuka*-style costume hanging on the wall attests to more extroverted moments. You will find no dungarees or diesel oil in this club, but rather a valuable resource for those of you who need it.

Open from 6 p.m. till 12 a.m.
Thursday to Tuesday. Closed on
Wednesday.
Hosono Bldg. 3F,
2-15-13 Shinjuku,
Shinjuku-ku.
(03) 3354-7923
¥¥¥¥

Les Girls and Boys

Torch Bar

Karaoke has recently become immensely popular in Tokyo's gay scene. If you are one of those people who needs so much alcohol to get the courage up to sing that by the time you do all the clubs are closed, this little bar should solve your problem. I have been there at five a.m. and everyone just seemed to be starting. As a gay bar, they are totally relaxed about accepting foreign and female customers, but you will find that most of the regulars are Japanese men. Unless you are an exceptional singer, you would not include this club on a list of gay pickup joints—other bars in the area will fill that need more satisfactorily. You are not obliged to sing, but as it stays open so late most customers discover some (deservedly) well-hidden talent, at which point you may wish you had a pair of earplugs with you. But hey, if you're out so late yourself, maybe it will sound OK. This is an excellent place to drop by if you just haven't had enough. The table charge is ¥500 and crooning is only ¥200/tune.

*Open from 8 p.m. till 5 a.m.
every day.
Sunny Co. Bldg. IF,
2-7-4 Shinjuku,
Shinjuku-ku.
(03) 3354-9156
¥¥*

Les Girls and Boys

Fuji

This was one of the first gay bars in Tokyo to gain some international notoriety through being listed in the early *Spartacus* series of guidebooks. A lot of new arrivals still come here first, but as soon as they plug into the scene, their patronage is attracted by other newer, more popular gay bars. The club is basically one largish, dimly-lit room with a central, mirror-backed bar surrounded by stools and a small, couched alcove in one corner. The incumbent manager, Maiki-san, does have a loyal following among his local and foreign friends, who often drop by midweek with a video to watch on the club's largish monitor. This extended neighborhood living room ambiance gives it a less desperate and more laid-back atmosphere than other clubs. When it is empty, single men tend to move on, but if you are with a large group of friends this would be an excellent place to party. It is more of a couples bar and one of the few that allows women to enter. This is a bar waiting for its atmosphere.

Open from 7:30 p.m. till 2:30 a.m. Sunday to Thursday, and till 3 a.m. on Friday and Saturday.
Sentofo Bldg. B1F,
2-12-16 Shinjuku,
Shinjuku-ku.
(03) 3354-2707
¥

Les Girls and Boys

Sunny

You will find this extremely friendly and unpretentious (if verging on run-down) lesbian *nomiya* on the same tiny back street in Shinjuku 2-chome that houses nearly all the establishments catering to this market. Sunny, the *mama-san* (though I should say *master-san* as she calls her female bar helper "the boy"), wears her hair short, keeps her sense of humor well-honed, and delivers a deep belly laugh whenever she feels the urge. You'll find no hands in front of faces in this bar. She also has a much more relaxed policy toward male customers than other lesbian haunts, allowing gay couples and men whom her female customers will vouch for to enter. In other words, no heterosexual predators or voyeurs allowed (but they let me in anyway). Frequenting this bar would be a very down-home way of gaining intro to this scene. Once the mandatory snack and charm fees have been added, your first drink will cost about ¥2,500 altogether, making it the cheapest lesbian bar in Tokyo.

Open from 8 p.m. till 5 a.m. Monday to Saturday, and till 3 a.m. on Sunday. Closed on 2nd and 3rd Sunday of the month. 2-15-8 Shinjuku 2F, Shinjuku-ku. (03) 3356-0368 ¥¥¥

Les Girls and Boys

Kusuo

This is a serious boys bar frequented by sporty, muscle-bound men with crew cuts. Kusuo is an abbreviation of Kyushu Otoko (Kyushu man). The men of this region are reportedly the strongest and bravest in Japan, but in this context it means butch. It has a dark, well-worn wooden interior with a central counter flanked by couches. You will be greeted, seated, and made welcome. The staff wear *happi* and *fundoshi* in the summer and, if you're lucky, one will give you a massage while chatting to you. The main appeal is its masculine, locker-room atmosphere, but since they introduced *karaoke*, a few camp patrons have started dropping by. The songs tend to be kitsch retro-Japanese tunes of the Pink Lady vein. This spoils the mood for the body boys, but if you know a song this could break the ice for you. It is more of a chat bar than a pickup joint, so little Japanese will go a long way. The first drink is ¥1,000 on the weekend (when it is best to get there early) and you pay as you leave.

Open from 8 p.m. till 3 a.m. (or till 2 a.m. if it's slow) Sunday to Thursday, and till 4 a.m. on Saturday.
Sunflower Bldg. 3F,
2-17-1 Shinjuku,
Shinjuku-ku.
(03) 3354-5050
¥

Les Girls and Boys

Zip

If you are interested in looking at young, good-looking boys, this club is pure chicken. You won't find a plusher interior in a 2-chome bar in which to watch them, either. Everything is finished in marble or wood and lit so that every surface shimmers softly. There is a bar down one side which leads you to a small seating and dancing area at the back, but the men who come here do so to see or be seen. The staff is very friendly and very handsome. This is look and don't touch territory. Foreigners are welcome, but the Japanese clientele are usually just not interested. Any unsuspecting *gaijin* who comes here, sees what he likes, and ends up unable to get it, would include this bar on a 2-chome night circuit for broken hearts. It is quite acceptable to drop by for a look. Newcomers will find it interesting to see just how cute Japanese boys can be, but they will also find it frustrating. If you know you're cute and to die for, you might score, but otherwise you'll only end up window shopping.

Open from 8 p.m. till 5 a.m. every day.
2-14-11 Shinjuku 1F, Shinjuku-ku.
(03) 3356-5029
¥

Madonna

The atmosphere and following of this club pleasantly bridges the gap between the Old Guard Mars Bar lesbians and the relatively rough and rowdy Sunny set. It is neat and comfortable and feels remarkably spacious when you consider its tiny dimensions. The *mama-san* is very stylish and friendly and mainly serves a similarly well-dressed and accessorized female clientele. Once again, no men are allowed. Not to be outdone by the current camp propensity for crooning *karaoke*, this appropriately-named lesbian bar offers their female counterparts the same opportunity. Madonna is not the exclusive domain of the red-blooded male population of this planet. She is just as much a sex symbol for the gay and lesbian communities. I wish I had a ¥1,000 for every time I've heard a Madonna song being butchered in a gay *karaoke* bar. At least these women sound better. The pricing system here also fits neatly between Mars and Sunny, with a ¥2,000 cover charge and drinks starting at ¥800.

Open from 9 p.m. till 5 a.m.
Monday to Saturday, and from 7
p.m. till 2 a.m. on Sunday.
Fujita Bldg. 1F,
2-15-13 Shinjuku,
Shinjuku-ku.
(03) 3354-1330
¥¥¥

Mellow Yellow

Once you have established a cultural foothold in Tokyo, you will be able to move around the city more freely. The longer you stay, the more you will become interested in places that new arrivals don't know about. You will want to flex your independence from the crowd and assert your awesome knowledge of the city by suggesting a drink in a great little bar you just happen to know. As is true of living anywhere, you know you have arrived when you walk in and the bartender greets you by name—a warm, comfortable relationship built up slowly over time.

Tokyo has hundreds of comfortable little bars with a no-fuss attitude and an extremely low-key clientele. Some of these establishments form the backbone of the modern Japanese dating circuit. They are descrete little places where you can take someone for a drink and a chat. You will find that in stark contrast to the drunken rowdiness of Japanese office parties and the cozy bonhomie of the local *nomiya*, the Japanese prefer to socialize intimately in a soothing, almost anonymous atmosphere—as do most people. There are also many bars aimed at a softer, more artistic clientele where people come to bathe in a quiet communal consciousness away from the glitzy superficiality of more upbeat nightlife haunts.

The burgeoning economy of the 1980s changed the way people partied in Tokyo. Not only did it attract more foreigners, it also meant that average local

Mellow Yellow

punters had more money at their disposal than their 1970s counterparts. They were also prepared to pay more to get something special. Many sophisticated little bars began popping up everywhere offering *plus alpha* services and style. There was a proliferation of members-only clubs charging hefty annual fees for the privilege of exclusivity. These have already closed down or changed hands and receded to usual levels, but the odor of affluence still hangs in some of these newer mellow bars.

The clubs listed here are not aimed at foreigners. Most are based on a foreign concept but all are aimed at local drinkers. Each establishment offers something unique, even if what makes it so is simply how this idea was reinterpreted for the local market. Whatever this concept might be, when a foreigner enters one of these bars, cultural osmosis goes full circle—you must play by local rules. The main focus of interaction is with the people you bring. These will be the kind of places you pop out to with a date or a mate for a tête-à-tête or quick drink.

You should be able to make a list of at least half a dozen bars that exactly suit your different moods. The bars listed here should add to your arsenal or help you assemble one. But remember, you will need to at least speak basic conversational Japanese to get by. You may find someone in attendance with the bare scrapings of English at their disposal, but there is no guarantee. With a few local graces and a smattering of Japanese, you will be able to sample some of these subtler delights of the city.

Cacciatora

This is a neo-beatnik bar and restaurant run and patronized by an interesting group of successful young Japanese designers, photographers, illustrators, and musicians. They have created a retro 50s-cum-60s cafe interior decorated with simplicity of style and injected with heavy doses of bright off-primary-colored formica and vinyl surfaces on all the furnishings. One entire wall features a fresh mural à la Joan Miro, which is highly representative of Tokyo's new beat generation's artistic leanings. This is definitely the sort of place to hang out in and drink if you feel cheated for having missed the Bohemian West Village days of New York. A random sample of the menu didn't turn up anything special, but as with other bar and restaurants that I have listed, you don't have to eat. The core group of this scene used to form a highly energetic band called Tokyo Rhythm Kings. If they ever regroup don't miss them—they really have a sense of humor and know how to entertain.

Open from 6 p.m. till 12 a.m.
Monday to Saturday. Closed on
Sunday.
Nishida Bldg. 2F,
1-18-2 Minami-ebisu,
Shibuya-ku.
(03) 3715-8218
¥

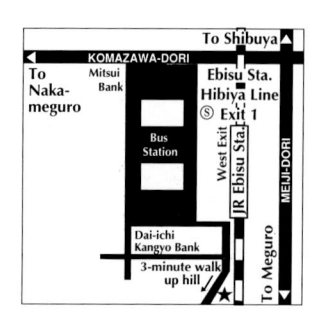

B.B. Gallery

The Japanese are generally stereotyped as being extremely conformist, but the few who manage to break this mold tend to become fiercely individualistic. Makoto Ohtaka is among these few. He is hard to pin down in terms of both what city and what business he might be in at any given moment. When he is in Tokyo, though, you'll find him at the controls of his uniquely designed and fabulously down-beat bar. He runs a rag trade from the premises by day and a deliciously quiet and laid-back bar at night. If you drop by after eight p.m., you will find that he has handed the keys over to an extremely soft young Japanese couple who manage the bar in his absence. His fantastic furniture gives this space a truly unique flavor. It looks great even if it isn't incredibly comfortable. If you're game you might try the giant pot-scourer suite or, better yet, the bathroom, which has to be seen to be believed. This is not a party place, but an excellent spot for a tête-à-tête or rendezvous.

Open from 7 p.m. till 4 a.m. every day.
1-10-25 Naka-meguro 1F, Meguro-ku.
(03) 3794-1877
¥¥

Kit Cat Club

Anybody who has ridden the Yamanote Line through Ebisu will probably have spotted the billboard for this bar from the train. Surprisingly few people have taken the chance and dropped in. This is probably because the name suggests an establishment much more sophisticated than it really is. Don't worry—it doesn't bite and neither does the bill! In fact, if you take the plunge you'll find a very cozy neighborhood haunt serving cheap eats cafeteria-style as you enter and booze from a bar in the corner. Another corner houses two pool tables, which are reasonably popular with those few local foreign residents who already know about them. Also, three chess boards are painted on one of the long eating tables, but no one is really taking advantage of them because you have to bring your own pieces. You are more than welcome to do so. This is nothing to cross town for, but if you live in the area, it would make a nice change from your four-mat room or another night in front of the TV.

Open from 5 p.m. till 1 a.m.
every day.
Daikoku Bldg. 2F,
1-8-14 Ebisu,
Shibuya-ku.
(03) 3444-5512
¥

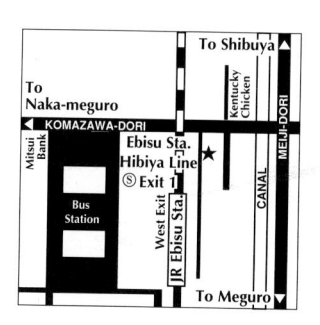

Mellow Yellow

Baccarat

The maze of little back streets that meander between Daikan-yama and Ebisu are becoming increasingly populated with curious bars. This one is perched on top of a building specifically designed to cater to this trend. Every floor houses some kind of bar or restaurant, but none are worth mentioning except this one. The interior is clean, modern, and warmly-lit. Equal emphasis has been given to the shadows to create a moody simplicity. All the furnishings have been carefully chosen and artfully arranged—and then messed up a little just for good measure. It is run by a young Japanese graphic designer and patronized by an interesting assortment of his hip young cohorts. As such, it would make a good place to discuss philosophy in the context of art (if your Japanese is up to it) or unwind with a drink after a hard day at the easel. This is not the sort of place to go if you're looking for some action. It should be thought of more as a lofty retreat from the tedium of the party rat race.

Open from 8 p.m. till 2 a.m. or so Monday to Saturday. Closed on Sunday.
Roob5 Bldg. 5F,
2-11-8 Nishi-ebisu,
Shibuya-ku.
(03) 3496-3072
¥

Exotica

When it first opened, this basement bar was a passable venue for a drink if the crowds at the original (and tiny) Ink Stick across the hall made live nights unbearable. The current version of the club, however, is a very pleasant hideaway in its own right. The concept for the interior is a fabulous juxtaposition of a bamboo forest within a concrete jungle. A rectangular bar in the center services the seamless line of bar stools facing it. All eyes face center-stage, where brightly-colored folksy highlights of various traditional Japanese *mingei* are interspersed among a large central bamboo cluster. Other similar details are scattered about. One wall is home to an enormous painting of a reclining blonde surrounded by similarly Japanesque objects, forming an interesting focal point. It is dimly lit and well serviced by discreet bar staff mainly catering to couples who wander in for a drink until four in the morning. There is an ¥800 cover charge and drinks start at the same price.

Open from 7 p.m. till 4 a.m.
every night.
Casa Grande Miwa Bldg. B1F,
7-5-11 Roppongi,
Minato-ku.
(03) 3403-1537
¥¥

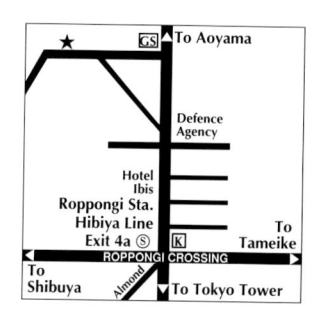

Never Never Land

Atmosphere and character are the major appeal of this charmingly low-key nook. It is decorated with a serendipitous assortment of knickknacks that lend it the warmth and feel of an earthy hippie kitchen, but in this case it's a bar. The owner, Matsuzaki-san, has been opening the doors of his homey hideaway to the drinkers and thinkers of Shimo-kitazawa for nearly 15 years. The main difference he has noticed in that time is that, starting a few years ago, his Japanese patrons began spending more money, frequently ordering cognac or calling the label on their bourbon. He has had to stock his bar accordingly. Though he has always had foreign friends, Never Never Land has only recently become popular with ghettoites. These days, it mostly caters to a firmly ensconced and mixed group of regulars. It is so tiny that there's not much room for new blood anyway. People come to chat or read or foot-tap to the Led Zeppelin-era music, which is definitely back in vogue at the top of this stairway.

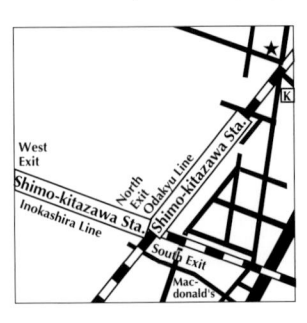

Open from 8 p.m. till 2 a.m. Sunday to Thursday, and till 3 a.m. on Friday and Saturday. Sometimes closes without warning.
3-20-1 Kitazawa 2F, Setagaya-ku.
(03) 3465-0737
¥

Berlin

The problem with a lot of bars in Shimo-kitazawa is their size. They are so small that sometimes it will just be impossible to jam even one extra midget-drinker in the door. As with everywhere else, this generally happens on the weekend. So if you've set your heart on a night out in Shimo but don't seem to be able to get in anywhere, this bar may prove to be a valuable solution. It is one of the lesser-known rock and grot dives in the area serving a largely Japanese clientele. The "rock and booze" tag on the sign outside sells it very short of the relatively sophisticated ambiance you will find inside. No unnecessary frills clutter the clean modern lines of its interior. The warm, woody tones of its furnishings give it a solid, comfortable atmosphere. A long row of *bottle-keeps* lining the shelf above the bar, some with labels artfully colored by the bar's more creative patrons, indicate a steady flow of regulars. For a bar that stays open until five o'clock every morning, it is incredibly clean and sane.

Open from 9 p.m. till 5 a.m.
every day.
Hon Kuito Bldg. 2F,
2-8-12 Kitazawa,
Setagaya-ku.
(03) 3485-0081
¥

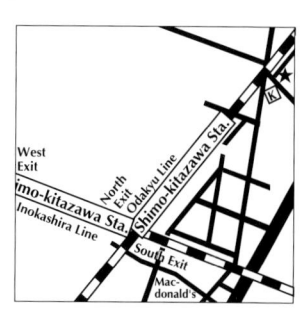

Trouble Peach

If a box of matches from this bar was your only clue to the night before, you would be excused for blushing. With a name like this and a picture of a leopard lolling around a giant butt-shaped peach, you might suspect that you had been lured into a no-panties bar. The word balloon coming out of the leopard's mouth proclaiming the name of its tiny six-seater counterpart downstairs, Eat a Peach, might make you think you're in even bigger trouble. Think again. It is just another sit-and-drink bar, but this one is mainly patronized by Japanese. Foreigners seem to prefer trying to squeeze into Eat a Peach, presumably so that they can write home with another "You'll never believe . . . " story—it really is insanely small. Upstairs is relatively spacious with dark rows of picnic tables peopled with groups of locals locked in conversational huddles, which gives it a vaguely conspiratorial air. The music here has more of an emphasis on jazz, even though they bill themselves as another "rock'n'roll beer hall."

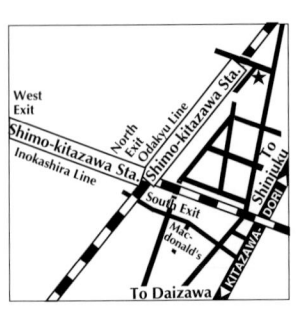

Open from 5 p.m. till 5 a.m. every day.
Kishida Bldg. 1F & 2F,
2-9-18 Kitazawa,
Setagaya-ku.
(03) 3460-1468
¥

Cay

The basement of the eye-catching Spiral Building in Aoyama houses this fanciful Thai restaurant-cum-bar. It has been around since the building first opened, but when all the staff quit en masse a few years ago, rumors were rife that it might close down. Except for a different set of smiling faces at the door and bar, however, it has survived intact. In fact, the only notable difference is that it closes earlier and it no longer enjoys the same cool and groovy following that it once attracted. The decor effectively creates a tropical hideaway atmosphere with leafy palm trees scattered about and mysterious back-lit silhouettes of rice-paddies and other generic Thai vistas set into the wall behind the long, winding bar. They still host live shows from time-to-time which can be anything from a variety of foreign ethnic groups to local Japanese acts, so check ahead for details. Live nights tend to be a little expensive—you'd be lucky to get away with paying under ¥10,000 including dinner.

Open from 6:30 p.m. till 11:30 p.m. Monday to Saturday. Closed on Sunday and holidays, except for special events. Spiral Bldg. B1F, 5-6-23 Minami-aoyama, Minato-ku. (03) 3498-5790 ¥/¥¥¥¥

Mellow Yellow

Tesoro

As far as food goes, this Spanish restaurant is pretty average—even for Tokyo. As a venue for a comfortable late-night drink, however, it is definitely worth knowing about. If you are trying to impress someone special and find yourself in this neighborhood, you may just score high points for suggesting a nightcap here. The interior was designed by a well-known local talent, Masami Matsui, who has created a very stylish and contemporary, neo-Mediterranean environment. Discreetly demur lighting and interesting roughly-sculpted metal braces along the walls create a pleasant feeling of intimacy at the tables. The plaster walls are inset with alcoves displaying earthy Spanish pottery and the ceiling is strung with rustic-looking strips of bamboo. The furnishings are fashionable yet comfortable. You can drop by for a drink at the solid rough-hewn slab of wood that serves as a bar just inside the door at any time. When the heat is off in the dining room, though, you can slip into either area.

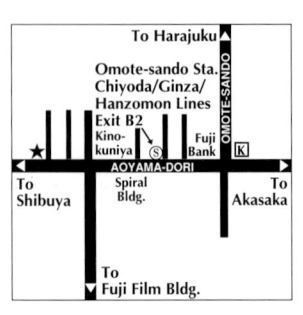

Open from 11 a.m. till 4 a.m. every day.
Citibank Bldg. B1F,
5-51 Jingumae,
Shibuya-ku.
(03) 3407-0192
¥/¥¥

Bar Replicant

As with other major party centers in Tokyo, Shimo-kitazawa features establishments that cater to every taste. If you are looking for flawless service in an ultra-sophisticated setting, Bar Replicant is a jewel. It is run by a former stage actor who was so impressed by the movie *Blade Runner* that he decided to name his bar after the film's terminally programmed androids, most notably portrayed by Rutger Hauer and Darryl Hannah. The interior is ultra-sleek and futuristic like the sort of bar in which Rachel may have preferred to meet Deckard. Two pleasant, well-groomed young men attend the bar to welcome you and take your orders—possibly Pleasure Models? This place looks so discrete and up-market from the street that my friend was reluctant to go in at first, fearing that it might be a hostess bar. However, you will find that most of the customers have some connection with the theater and that the bill is surprisingly cheap. They also serve some very tasty and well-presented snacks.

Open from 7 p.m. till 2 a.m. Monday to Saturday, and till 12 a.m. on holidays. Closed on Sunday.
Sangyu Bldg. 2F,
2-9-3 Kitazawa,
Setagaya-ku.
(03) 3466-3773
¥/¥¥

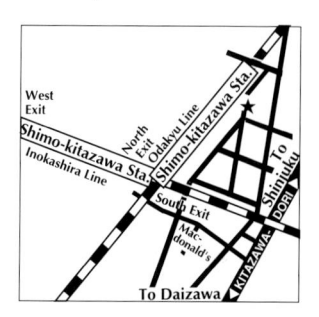

Mellow Yellow

Stomp

With a name like this, one would expect to find a steamy jampacked live house full of hordes of screaming teenagers slam dancing wildly inside. Instead, it's a very laid-back rhythm-and-blues bar where some of Shimo-kitazawa's more mature patrons wander in from the night to listen to their favorite music. The bartender will play requests if he can find them easily enough in their extensive record collection. A few classic covers are dimly spot-lit above the bar, but otherwise the interior exudes a sort of furry darkness, like walking into a black-on-black velvet painting. The walls are actually red brick and the ceiling is a rough-textured plaster—details which are hard to discern, but once you do, you're sure that you would rather not see them with the lights on. There are only two tables and a few bar stools, so an *ai-seki* arrangement is observed with the seating. Some people peep through the door but move on if they feel it is too crowded, as if this is an unspoken rule.

*Open from 7 p.m. till 5 a.m.
every day.
Sato Bldg. B1F,
2-11-4 Kitazawa,
Setagaya-ku.
(03) 3412-4940
¥*

B-girl

When somebody tells you that they know a great little bar in Mejiro that stays open all night, you can be excused for reacting cautiously. The ever-expanding party centers to Mejiro's north and south, Ikebukuro and Takada-no-baba, respectively, don't even have it that good. But it's true and it's an excellent find for anyone living in the area. At first you may feel like you've accidentally stumbled into someone's reading room, as the entry is piled high with stacks of magazines, books, and games. Once through this jumble, however, the interior spreads out into comfy, tabled corners where couples chat or loners hunch over comic books. It is warm, friendly, and very low-key. Large picture windows overlook the busy Yamate/Mejiro-dori intersection below, and if you've forgotten to pick up some groceries, there's a 24-hour convenience store downstairs. It is busy until 11 p.m., when people clear out for trains, and then kicks in again around two a.m., when locals start dropping by.

Open from 6 p.m. till 5 a.m.
every day.
1-27-17 Naka-ochiai 2F,
Shinjuku-ku.
(03) 3954-4294
¥

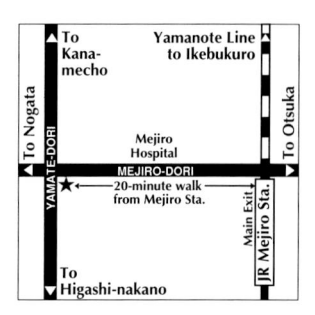

Mellow Yellow

Ça va, ça va

This ultra-sophisticated bar would be better placed on the Ginza or in a five-star hotel than between a Korean and Chinese restaurant on a grotty backstreet in Shinjuku. The bartenders are obviously trained professionals, who are discreet of action and unobtrusively attentive. The lighting is arranged so that if they take a half-step back from the counter, they disappear into shadow—as all good bartenders should. The drinks menu is an education in itself, with over 100 malt Scotch whiskeys listed according to their highland region and all liqueurs and other spirits listed according to their country of origin. One of the cheapest Scotches is a 12-year-old Islay Malt going for ¥1,100. They go up in price from there to a 1961 Glenfarclas Speyside single malt for ¥6,500 a shot, but no one has been tempted yet. Orange juice is freshly squeezed and served in a long-stemmed glass. The mixed nuts even include a few macadamias. For serious connoisseurs (with pocketbooks to match).

Open from 7 p.m. till 3 a.m. Monday to Saturday. Closed on Sunday and holidays. Gomeikan Bldg. B1F, 3-3-9 Shinjuku, Shinjuku-ku. (03) 3353-4650 ¥¥

Lupin

This was one of Tokyo's first basement bars when it opened in 1928. The background details in a few old photos taken in the bar's early days, including one of noted Japanese author Osamu Dazai, would indicate that not much has changed since then. The high average age of the bar help also indicates a low turnover in staff for the last 20 years and adds another frozen-in-time aspect to the atmosphere. A long and extremely solid wooden bar, from the days when wood was wood and plastic was unheard of, runs the length of the interior and some authentic church pews create a couple of booths off to one side. The subdued lighting and the settled, solid feeling of the decor give the place a pleasant, dingy warmth. Not only old-timers come here. It is also popular with young office workers who turn up en masse after dinner. Its unique atmosphere is obviously the main attraction, though price-wise it is also cheaper than the bulk of the Ginza's other establishments.

Open from 5:30 p.m. till 11:30 p.m. Monday to Saturday. Closed on Sunday and holidays. Tsukamoto Fudosan Bldg. B1F, 5-5-11 Ginza, Chuo-ku. (03) 3571-0750 ¥¥

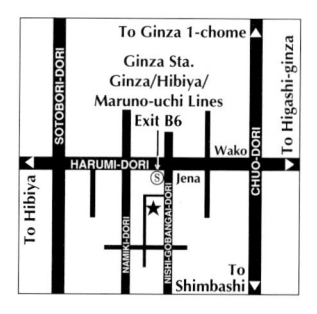

Mellow Yellow

Mandalaya

Tucked away on a tiny lane off Shinjuku-dori near the main Yotsuya crossing, this neighborhood hangout is full of many pleasant surprises. For a start, they sell my favorite Belgian beer, Chimay, but only the red label, which I prefer to the blue label, and only in small bottles, or "grenades" as I like to call them. They also offer an extensive menu, but only in Japanese, which features an across-the-board selection of tasty foods from various ethnic origins, but you are not obliged to eat. The staff is very friendly and helpful, and while they are not all teenagers, they are definitely young at heart. The interior is simple yet warm with a wooden floor and furnishings, to which the odd Chinese wine jeroboam adds an earthy touch. The music is an excellent mix of classic funk, blues, and rock, which varies according to whoever is changing the tape but which always seems to hit the spot. This is a cool little place which everybody living in the Yotsuya area should know about.

Open from 6 p.m. till 2 a.m.
Monday to Saturday. Closed on
Sunday and holidays.
Ueno KG Bldg. B1F,
1-23 Yotsuya,
Shinjuku-ku.
(03) 3353-3282
¥

Zorro

A dimly lit back street in Roppongi houses this extremely sophisticated two-story establishment. In contrast to its immediate neighborhood, it is very bright and airy with a Spanish-style *tappas* bar on the first floor. The interior is bathed in the reflected warmth of its peach-colored walls and subtly arranged lighting. A long sweeping bar is fronted by black wire-framed stools and temptingly displays the daily specials of food and wine. The rest of this enormous space is filled out with clusters of tables and chairs and earthy hacienda-type details. Over 40 kinds of sherry and 20 kinds of *cava* (Spanish sparkling wine) are available, including Cordon Brut Negro for ¥4,000 a bottle. The house wine goes for ¥800 a glass. Half a dozen kinds of *tappas* are available for ¥600 a plate. If your gastric juices get too excited you can slip downstairs and sample something from the Madrid-style menu in the restaurant. This is an excellent spot to drop by for a snack and a drink.

Open from 11:30 a.m. till 2 p.m. for lunch and from 5:30 p.m. till 11 p.m. for dinner Monday to Saturday. Closed on Sunday and holidays.
A.T. Bldg. 1F & B1F,
4-12-2 Roppongi,
Minato-ku.
(03) 3423-3500
¥¥

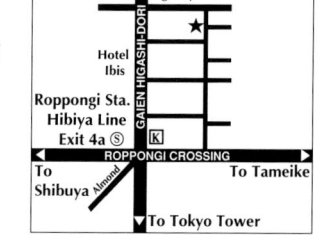

Mellow Yellow

Penthouse

You have probably walked past the entrance to this bar a hundred times and thought the name implied a different sort of establishment. It is, in fact, a very homey nest filled with potted plants and decorated with knickknacks from all over Southeast Asia. Many of these are rather amusingly raunchy, but that is as close as you'll come to any similarity with the magazine of the same name. It is perched precariously at the very top of a narrow building in Roppongi, which affords it excellent views of the party mecca below. A now middle-aged and earthy Japanese couple have been running this highrise oasis for over 15 years. The *master-san* used to visit Bali regularly in his younger days for the surf. He also keeps his pet raccoon, Mariko-chan, firmly ensconced at the bar. For the most part she is content to quietly doze, but if you say hello be careful as she likes to scratch and sniff. The *master-san* often chews up a cracker with some orange juice and passes it to her mouth-to-mouth. Very cozy.

Open from 6 p.m. till 2 a.m. Monday to Saturday. Closed on Sunday and holidays. Sansei Kaikan 9F, 7-14-2 Roppongi, Minato-ku. (03) 3405-4588/3405-9758 ¥

Mon

Many of you may remember Mon as a poky little Japanese-style *nomiya* incongruously nestled in between modern concrete-and-chrome buildings in the heart of Shibuya. If you haven't dropped by for a while, you are in for a big surprise. Gone are the sliding doors and wooden rafters. In their place, and more in keeping with the neighborhood, is—you guessed it—a modern concrete-and-chrome building. It is now three pristinely modern floors catering to a very *Shibu-kaji* set of drinkers. Mon: The Whales of August in the first floor basement is set up like a shot bar, while Mon (proper) on the first floor and Mon: Poru Bari (Port Variation) on the second floor function more like typical *nomiya*. The only thing the same is the aging owner, who now runs around busying himself between floors instead of being posted at what was his usual mission-control post behind the till. It's hard not to heave a huge sigh of nostalgia at the passing of the old Mon from our midst.

B1F and 2F open from 5 p.m. till 4 a.m. every day. 1F open from 5 p.m. till 12 a.m. Monday to Saturday, and closed on Sunday. 28-13 Udagawa-cho, Shibuya-ku.
B1F: (03) 3476-7238
1F: (03) 3476-7236
2F: (03) 3476-7237
¥

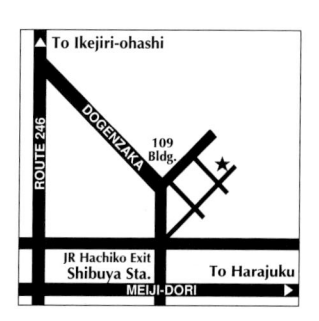

Shanghai

From time to time, we all need a convenient place to meet for a quiet chat and a drink. Ebisu is not lacking in establishments to meet this need, but we all get a little sick of those hard to find places that have you tearing you hair out by the time you get there, or those bland coffee-shop chains that abound everywhere. This bar is right next to the station and it has the sort of pleasant modern interior that makes you think it might be expensive—but it's not. During the week, it is mainly patronized by Japanese company employees who come here to ruminate over the day's events at the office. On the weekend, however, it can sometimes take on a ghetto aspect as it is right downstairs from Bodeguita, which closes around midnight leaving many people wound up and wondering where to go next. This is the first place they see when they hit the street. In any case, if you have to meet someone in Ebisu for a few beers and don't feel like making a big night out of it, you should try this bar.

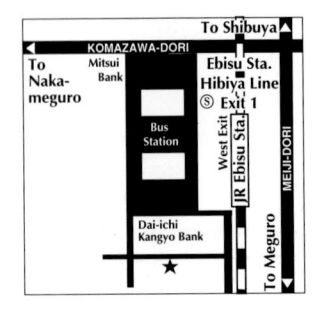

Open from 8 a.m. (for coffee, beer, and wine) and from 6 p.m. (full bar) till 2 a.m. Monday to Saturday, and till 11:30 p.m. on Sunday and holidays.
New Life Ebisu Bldg. 1F,
1-7-8 Ebisu,
Shibuya-ku.
(03) 3715-2207
¥

Billboard

There are very few bars in Shibuya that offer something more interesting and intimate than a disco or standard neon-lit watering hole. This cozy little downstairs bar has potential, though. Like-minded refugees from the tinsel town above drop by to sit and sip and listen to rock and blues classics. These tunes are delivered through excellent JBL Sound Power speakers, but the music is not so loud that you can't hear each other talk. It is comfortable and earthy with a heavy emphasis on wood and old pub mirrors advertising classic quaffs line the walls. A life-size superman sculpture somehow manages to squeeze into a corner of the ceiling and a few antique-looking objects lie scattered about. All of these things are shrouded in the warm, rosy glow from stained-glass lampshades. In some ways it is nothing special, but it does seem to have a lot more soul and class than other Shibuya bars. It is probably best used as a place to grab a few drinks before heading home after dinner.

Open from 11 a.m. till 11:30 p.m. Sunday to Thursday, and till 1 a.m. on Friday, Saturday, and holiday eves.
Edoya Bldg. B1F,
25-1 Udagawa-cho,
Shibuya-ku.
(03) 3464-9208
¥

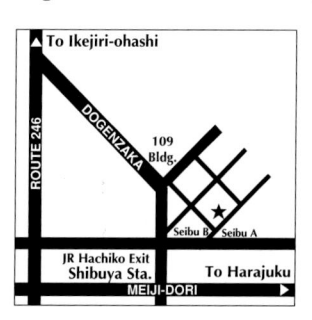

Le Sejour

This is a very chic hideaway which has been very cleverly designed to create various moods and functions within a limited space. Without being cluttered or overdone, there are distinct drinking, eating, and lounging areas. One corner even includes a cozy little tatami room. Two large color monitors are mounted on wheels so that you can watch a video from wherever you decide to get comfortable, though this would preferably be on one of the couches. One small drawback is that they only offer a limited range of mostly horror movies. A couple of sets of cordless headphones are also available so that you don't have to disturb (or be disturbed by) other customers while watching. These are a definite plus when it starts getting crowded in the early hours of the morning. The cocktail menu reads like a teenager's diary—I tried Sex On The Beach (very refreshing) followed by an Orgasm (a little disappointing as I don't like Amaretto). The spaghetti was quite tasty, too.

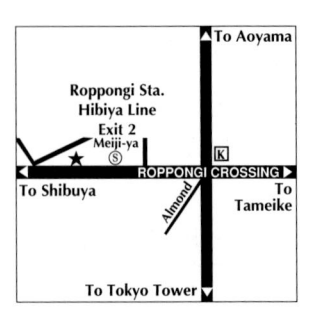

Open from 6 p.m. till 6 a.m. Monday to Saturday, and till 2 a.m. on Sunday and holidays. Kaneko Bldg. #1 3F, 7-18-13 Roppongi, Minato-ku.
(03) 3423-8260
¥¥

4 Play Ground

James Lappin is one of the few foreigners who has so far succeeded in opening his own bar in Tokyo. The result is unique in every way. The walls are covered in day-glo scenes of comic book machismo from the poke-your-eyes-out, blow-your-brains-out, and grind-the-rest-into-a-pulp school of cartoonery. The beer spigot is capped off with a dildo, which James pulls rather timidly (unless you point this out to him which results in a predictable display of extroversion). The clientele are mostly Japanese with a heavy bias toward cute girls and agile men interested in Thai kick-boxing—both passions of James'. There is no cover charge but drinks are a little expensive. They start at ¥800 but mostly go for around ¥1,000. However, he does give you a good shot in a cocktail and also makes an excellent blue margarita. His intense but generally good-natured manner has already attracted a rather colorful array of bar flys. Definitely worth the price of a cocktail (or three).

Open from 7 p.m. till 2:30 a.m.
Monday to Saturday. Closed on
Sunday and sometimes for
private parties.
Hasshin Bldg. B1F,
2-25-12 Nishi-azabu,
Minato-ku.
(03) 5466-1945
¥/¥¥

Wild Cards

Various fates destin a bar or club to be thrown in with the Wild Cards. Mostly they are misfits that have defied categorization by having created their own genre. Most of these genre-bender bars have developed and survived on the strength of a particular passion or personality trait of their creator. These eccentric *mamas* and *masters* usually decided to start their own club because no one else was catering to their needs or those of their customers. They set up shop and ended up creating their own specialized niche tucked away in an undefined corner of Tokyo's nighttime fabric. Hostess bars are a dime a dozen, but Henry Miller's last wife Hoki has a unique story and a place to tell it. Then there is George whose love of soul has created a delightfully eccentric hole-in-the-wall, and Setsuko-san whose funky little *nomiya* forms the backbone of Shimo-kitazawa's late night drinking circuit. These and other bars like them are cherished oases of originality that nobody could or would want to imitate.

Then there are the faded fad bars. The past decade has seen a proliferation of nightlife fads in Tokyo. The city has wrestled with rashes of goldfish-bowl bars, shot bars, pool halls, casinos, and, most recently, sports bars. The first bar opens and then others quickly follow suit. Most of them come into existence on the crest of the trend, and most of them are washed away once the wave breaks. Some survivors manage

Wild Cards

to brace themselves against these changing tides. This is usually because the fad itself addressed a valid nightlife concept which over time caters to a smaller, but still interested, clientele. Taken collectively, they represent a mixed bag of theme bars that can only be considered as a group because they share the same faddish origins. These smoldering embers of what was once hot can also be conveniently swept into the Wild Cards' carryall.

Then there are the concept bars. The most prolific of these are 60s rock'n'roll memorabilia bars. Most people have heard of the Cavern Club which features a Beatles look-alike band who sing perfect harmony to a foot-tapping audience. It's not bad value but it is very prepackaged, just like the Kentos chain of clubs that feature local *lock'n'loll* outfits of radically varying ability. These clubs are easily accessed, so rather than recommend them I suggest trying some seedier, offbeat bars like Rolling Stone and Pub Elvis. Or in a different vein, try a night in *Casablanca* at Bogey's Bar.

Then there are specialist bars, which cater to extremely specific markets. European beer bars could be regarded as part of the overall trend toward sophistication in the 1980s, but they will survive because they have generated a genuine interest in their brews. Many foreigners can't read Japanese so a night out singing *karaoke* can be extremely frustrating. If so, try Smash Hits which features a comprehensive list of English-language songs. Or how about a little tits and glit at a transsexual cabaret? Whatever it is, if it doesn't fit neatly into a category, you'll find it here.

Bogey's Bar

This is a replica of Rick's Café Américain from the classic Humphry Bogart and Ingrid Bergman movie, *Casablanca*. The stucco arches, the palm trees, the lethargically revolving ceiling fans—you'll find them all here. You will also find a replica of the film's upright piano, across which Bogey never leans to deliver the frequently misquoted line, "Play it again, Sam." It is put to good use on Friday and Saturday night to play songs from the movie's score. There is also an old Sonora wind-up gramophone and a stack of ancient Bakerlite records complete with scratches and crackles, through which you can occasionally discern a big-band tune recorded in Turkish. A photograph of Lauren Bacall, taken when she visited the club a few years ago, is prominently displayed on the bar. This is not a place for wild revelry (Dejavu is right downstairs if that's what you want), but rather a nostalgic setting for a whiff of an imaginary world of shady gangsters and femme fatales. BYO imagination.

Open from 6 p.m. till 5 a.m. Monday to Saturday, and till 2 a.m. on Sunday and holidays. Togensha #2 Bldg. 2F, 3-15-24 Roppongi, Minato-ku.
(03) 3478-1997/1998
¥

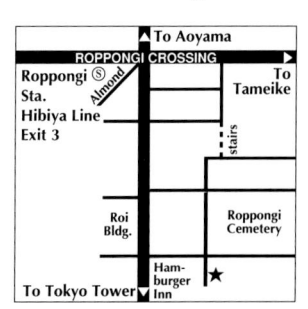

Smash Hits

Have you ever wished those awful *karaoke* bars that your coworkers insist on hauling you off to had the kind of songs you really wouldn't mind singing? You know, something with a little more nostalgia or soul, or an irresistible top 40 hit that is so firmly etched in your brain that you can't help singing along anyway? Next time you find yourself being bodily propelled toward a collision with a microphone, suggest this fab, mini concert-hall. It has the most comprehensive English song list in Tokyo. This is not a good venue if you're shy—the mike stands are mounted on a real stage faced by tiered seating, so everybody in the 30-seater house has an excellent view of the proceedings. The staff will energetically encourage everyone to be famous for five minutes, so if you scare easily, you should insist on having the mike brought to you on remote. The decor has a heavy emphasis on perspex and plastic with all the seating, including the toilet, made out of heavy see-through studded vinyl.

Open from 8 p.m. till 5 a.m. Monday to Saturday. Closed on Sunday and holidays. M2 Hiroo Bldg. B1F, 5-2-26 Hiroo, Shibuya-ku. (03) 3444-0432 ¥¥¥

Brussels, Kanda

Three tiny wedge-shaped floors stacked one on top of the other create this poky but popular Belgian beer bar. They serve a wide variety of fine European beers to connoisseurs and the curious alike. Among others, you can try Bass Pale Ale and seasonal German beers, but the main focus is on Belgian brews. I have seen Americans drinking Czechoslovakian Budweiser be pleasantly surprised. In their country it is tagged as the "King of Beers," but in Czechoslovakia the original ale was always the "Beer of Kings." Some drinkers drop by just for the alcohol content, which can sometimes run as high as ten percent. The staff is friendly and efficient, and serve a small range of snacks, including delicious pita-bread sandwiches. You will definitely need something to soak up the effect of these often potent brews or suffer the conse-quences the next day. It is very mellow early in the evening, but if a few foreingers are still holding up the bar toward midnight, a ghetto aspect can set in.

Open from 5:30 p.m. till 2 a.m.
Monday to Friday, and till 11
p.m. on Saturday. Closed on
Sunday.
3-16-1 Kanda Ogawamachi,
Chiyoda-ku.
(03) 3233-4247
¥/¥¥

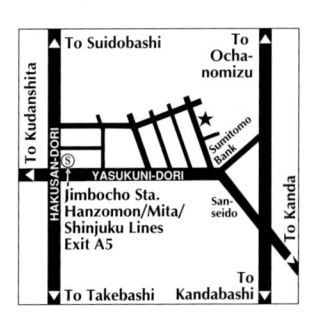

Brussels, Yaraicho

A quiet, nondescript street off Kagura-zaka leads you to the door of this second branch of the Brussels' duo. It lacks some of the atmosphere and quaintness of the Kanda branch and it hasn't yet gained the same following, but you will find the same fine selection of Belgian and other European brews available. It is one largish room with windows overlooking the street and a bar down one side faced by a dozen stools. Three long wooden tables fill out the rest of the space, but you will end up sharing these as people wander in and the place slowly begins to fill up throughout the evening. It is less manic than the original branch and therefore offers a more pleasant, relaxed atmosphere. But, because this branch has not yet gained the same notoriety, they are less prepared for catering to crowds. So, if one drops by, you may find that they have run out of food. Their supplies of beer, though, seem endless. The bartenders will sometimes call an early close if business is slow around midnight.

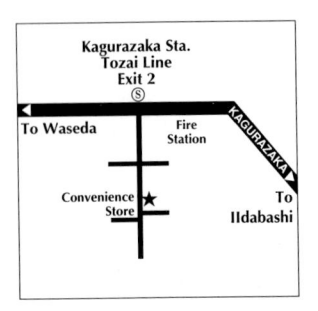

Open from 5:30 p.m. till 2 a.m. Monday to Friday, and from 11:30 a.m. till 11 p.m. on Saturday. Closed on Sunday. 75 Yaraicho, Shinjuku-ku. (03) 3235-1890 ¥/¥¥

Market

This is a grass-roots hole in the wall on the established late-night Shimo-kitazawa drinking circuit. It is truly unique in many ways. Firstly, it doesn't really have a name. Foreigners nickname it Market because it is located in the local Kitazawa market area. If you really push the locals for a name, they'll tell you something like Odenya Setsuko because it is an *odenya* and it is run by the ever-mirthful and well-seasoned Setsuko-san. Secondly, the shop itself only seats about five people. When all the other businesses nearby are roller-doored shut at night, Setsuko-san sets out the odd tarpaulin and some donut-shaped stools, and people create their own camp in the maze of streets around his shop. Patrons range from young rockers and punks in all their gear waiting for the first train, to locals just dropping by for a drink on the way home. Finally, asking Setsuko-san for the address and phone number solicited nothing but laughter—from both himself and his customers.

Open from 8 p.m. till your last order.
No address and no phone.
Ask where the market is around the north exit of the station and follow the map from there.
¥

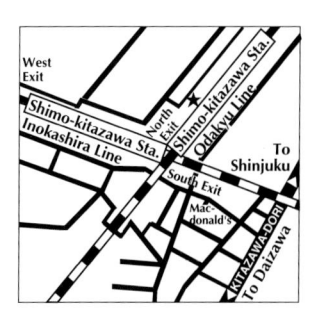

Café de Copain

If you're into watching feature films for the price of a drink, this place is not bad value. It is divided into three parts. To the right as you enter is a typical coffee-shop corner with a stack of magazines and a big screen, if you really want to watch the movie. In the center is a bar for hanging out and drinking, behind which are several small monitors showing the film without sound. To the left is a dimly lit, couched area which also features a large screen for the film, but has another intriguing function. It is a place where couples come to gently grope. We're not talking teenagers, either. There was a 20-something and a 30-something couple at it when I entered. Although it is far more comfortable than the coffee-shop end, you feel a little uncomfortable crunching too loudly on your rice puffs or calling the waitress over for a drink. That is, unless you have brought somebody to press the flesh with, in which case the bar goodies won't particularly interest you anyway.

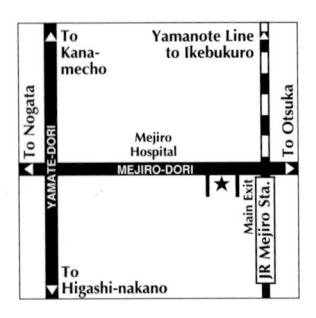

Open from 6 p.m. till 2 a.m. Monday to Saturday, and till 12 a.m. on Sunday (but sometimes closed).
Yutaka Bldg. 2F,
3-5-11 Mejiro,
Toshima-ku.
(03) 3952-4953
¥

Dr. Jeekahn's

Six floors of fanciful, futuristic architecture await the visitor to this adult playground. It costs ¥1,000 to enter, but after that you pay as you go on each floor. The entrance, or Venture Quad, houses a bar down one side. Planet Septon, on the second floor, features a walk-through laser-target game for ¥1,000. As well as a mean looking laser rifle, you get to wear a snazzy vest that somehow even makes a *salaryman* look like a cool, killer cyborg. Gammon, on the third floor, is a ¥1,000-minimum stake electronic casino featuring slot machines, poker, blackjack, roulette, and an extremely popular mechanical derby. Any winnings will be credited for your next visit. Hydrotto, on the fourth floor, is a Jules Verne underwater-theme restaurant— not bad if you're bored with eating in the 20th century (and cheap, too). Paladrome, on the fifth floor, has a bar and stage for performances under a domed, optical-fiber encrusted ceiling. The Doctor's Study overlooks this floor from a mezzanine above.

Open from 6 p.m. till 12 a.m. Monday to Friday, from 1 p.m. till 12 a.m. on Saturday, and from 1 p.m. till 11 p.m. on Sunday.
2-4 Maruyama-cho, Shibuya-ku.
(03) 3476-7811
¥¥

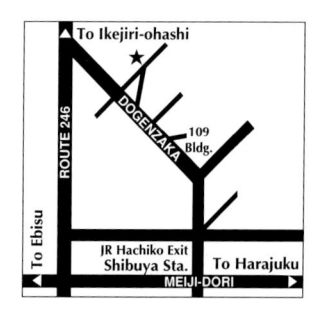

Petit Château

Tokyo is well-endowed with tacky cabarets featuring dancers in skimpy glitter costumes and yards of flouncing feathers. Petit Chateau is one but with a small difference—all the performers are *new-halves* (or transsexuals, as we would say in English). Some of the girls are so beautiful that you can't believe that they weren't born this way, especially the club's much-touted and stunning Seiko-san. It is sometimes possible to guess their origins by the classic telltale signs of the Adam's apple, hands, and voice (especially when they sing *karaoke* between floorshows). Without this kind of close scrutiny, even the most red-blooded male would be fooled (at least temporarily) into believing that he is being entertained by real women. It is extremely popular with mostly straight male and female customers and is always crowded in spite of the fact that it is prohibitively expensive—¥25,000 just to get in. A small bottle of beer is ¥1,000 and the cheapest bottle of whiskey is ¥20,000.

Open from 11 p.m. till 5 a.m. Monday to Saturday with shows at 2 a.m. and 4 a.m. Closed on Sunday and holidays.
Koyama Bldg. B1F,
3-1-19 Nishi-azabu,
Minato-ku.
(03) 3408-0204
¥¥¥¥¥¥¥¥¥¥¥¥¥¥¥¥¥¥¥¥¥¥¥¥¥
(more if you drink whiskey!)

Billy Barew's Beer Bar

The majority of Tokyo's bars are small. This imported beer bar is best described as miniscule, but the focus of the brews that they sell is global. I would be surprised if you didn't find your home-country's ale in stock. In spite of its size, it is very smart with tailor-made wooden booths down one side and a bar down the other. The narrow passage in between ostensibly leads to the bathroom, but when it gets packed to capacity on the weekend, its function as such becomes a moot point. It is well worth the struggle to make it through and check out the hologram inside, which acts as an incentive to get you there. The staff is rather interesting, being either martial-arts enthusiasts or Nepalese or both. Because of this unusual ethnic influence, they also serve some very tasty snacks. It is frequented by fresh-faced academics from the various universities nearby and an endless supply of young Japanese women. The weekend draws more of a ghetto crowd, but otherwise it is fairly laid-back.

Open from 5 p.m. till 12 a.m.
Monday to Thursday, and till 2
a.m. on Friday and Saturday.
Closed on Sunday and holidays.
1-17-10 Takada-no-baba,
Shinjuku-ku.
(03) 3209-0952
¥/¥¥

George's

This is a tiny corridor of a bar no wider than two tatami which clings almost desperately to one corner of the enormous Self Defense Headquarters block in Roppongi. George, the *mama-san*, is an avid soul enthusiast who opened this bar for her own amusement almost 30 years ago. Her jukebox is well stocked with whatever she has chosen to install from the 20,000-record plus collection of 45s that she has stockpiled at her home. Some old-time favorites are wearing thin with crackles these days, but that just adds to the charm of this place. It is a bit pricey, though, at ¥200 a tune. The walls are completely covered in nicoteen-coated promo shots and album covers of and by anyone George has liked or met over the past few decades. You can tell who's been there most recently by the color. This curious shrine to soul is well-known in Motown industry circles, but I've never been lucky enough to share a drink with any of the mega-stars who've added their signature to the wallpaper.

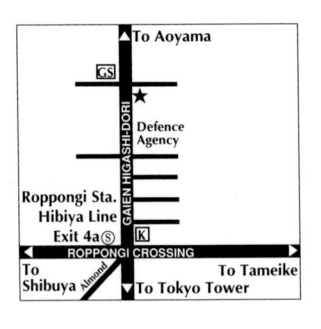

Opens whenever George is ready (but usually around 9 p.m.) and ditto for closing (but usually late, late, late).
7-55-9 Roppongi, Minato-ku.
(03) 3405-9049
¥/¥¥

Heavy Foot

Kagurazaka has all the usual *aka-cho-chin* and *snack* bars that you find in any old part of Tokyo, but it has only recently begun to attract Western-style establishments. It is literally and figuratively at the dead center of town, though the future promises to be brighter for this prime location. In the meantime, what better use could you put it to than parking half a pink Cadillac out on the pavement and opening a subterranean 60s "American space"? The back seat of the Cadie nestles up to a table inside and steals the limelight from all the other theme junk that lines the walls. The bartenders are all groovy young Japanese rock'n'rollers and the patrons are the sort of people who just don't want to go to a *snack* bar or be stung with an outrageous cover charge. There is an original Wurlitzer jukebox with some classic 45s spinning nonstop all night. It only costs ¥100 for three songs, but with only 30-odd selections available, you get to know them all a little too well. Not bad for a drink with your work buddies.

Open from 6 p.m. till 4 a.m.
Monday to Saturday.
Closed on Sunday.
M.S.K. Bldg. B1F,
6-38 Kagurazaka,
Shinjuku-ku.
(03) 3260-1961
¥

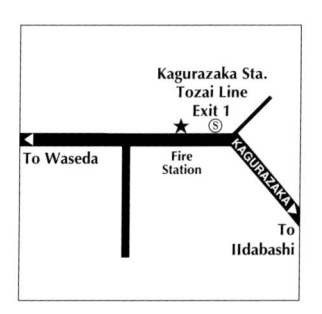

Pub Elvis

Yes, Tokyo has its own shrine posing as a club dedicated to the memory of The King. I know I wouldn't be impressed if I were his ghost—it's actually a rather shabby little *karaoke* bar, but the staff is very friendly and you don't have to sing. If you are tempted to, you will find many Presley classics on the song list (try [*sic*] "Cring in the Chapel" or "Blue Swede Shoes") among other moody favorites (like Otis Redding's "Dog of the Bay"). When no one is up at the mike, endless hours of Elvis videos flow from the monitors, including a good documentary from American TV. The menu offers an Elvis cocktail made from vodka, cherry brandy, and tonic. The *master-san* admits it has nothing to do with The King's favorite drink, but he says it's *oishii* and so was Elvis. They feature a live 50s band on Tuesday night. There is an ¥800 cover charge every night (but you get a free snack if you arrive before seven p.m.) and a ten percent service charge after midnight, but songs are only ¥200 a throw.

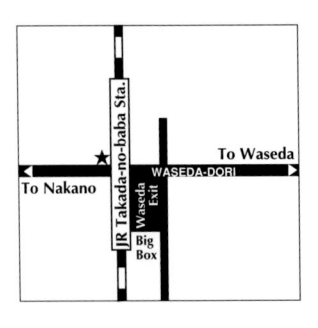

Open from 6 p.m. till 2 a.m. Monday to Saturday. Closed on Sunday and holidays. Tack Eleven Bldg. 2F, 2-19-7 Takada-no-baba, Shinjuku-ku. (03) 3232-0073 ¥¥

Star Bank

This is an intriguing bar to discover as it is well off the usual Roppongi party track. Also, business obviously isn't suffering, in spite of its location. When you enter, you will find a spacious and well-appointed club with a black-and-white checkered floor, a few palm trees scattered about, and long rows of glistening bottles behind the well-stocked bar. You will also find efficient, friendly, well-tailored waiters servicing tables of well-to-do Japanese professionals—so what, right? Well, as with many bars in Tokyo, what gives it an edge is the owner. Danny looks like a Japanese version of Wild Bill Hickok, with his long, slightly graying hair caught in a ponytail and handlebars on his mustache like the ones on his Harley Davidson parked out front. He is a real frontiersman and every bit as suspicious of strangers. His idea of a good time is flogging his hog on the highways of America. The contrast with his customers is stark—presumably they get a kick out of living his life vicariously for a night.

Open from 7 p.m. till 2 a.m.
Monday to Saturday. Closed on
Sunday and holidays.
City Azabu Bldg. 2F,
3-12-10 Azabu-juban,
Minato-ku.
(03) 3453-4177
¥

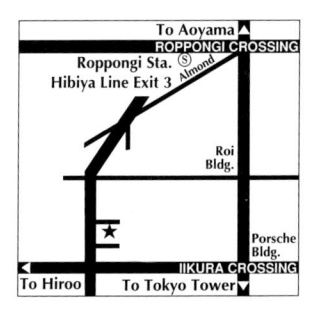

Tropic of Cancer

Hostess bars are a dime a dozen in Tokyo. What sets this one apart is the *mama-san*, Hoki. Her story, which begins with her crazy, fun-filled days as a piano player in San Francisco, where Henry Miller first met and fell in love with her, to her subsequent relocation to Tokyo after his death, is sadly moving and seldom fully told. Instead, she flings the doors of her club wide open and invites her customers inside to sip fine congnac and forget. She employs a small group of *gaijin* hostesses to help her entertain and a piano player to deliver brief but sweet sets throughout the night. She seldom takes to the ivories these days, but will occasionally do so if she is coerced strongly enough. If you drop by with a group, you will receive the usual hostess services and fees, but if you drop by with a date, you will be left discreetly undisturbed and with only a nominal fee added to the price of your drinks. Happy hour is from seven p.m. until nine p.m., after which the live music begins.

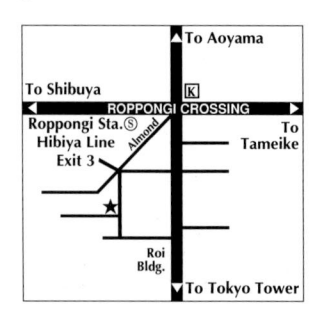

Open from 7 p.m. till 2 a.m. Monday to Saturday. Closed on Sunday and holidays. Reine Roppongi Bldg. 4F, 5-3-4 Roppongi, Minato-ku. (03) 5410-4737 ¥¥/¥¥¥¥

NFL Experience

The most obnoxious nightlife trend to emerge in Tokyo recently is a rash of sports bars. This one is housed in the fancy Beam Building in Shibuya, which is itself part of a trendy rash of bubble buildings—those wildly phantasmagoric architectural monuments built during Japan's once ballooning bubble economy of the late 80s. You will find this squeaky-clean-as-a-new-pair-of-Nikes bar in the basement. The floor is covered in Astro-turf and all the furniture is of the pressed-plastic outdoor mold. Just in case these tacky accouterments don't tip you off to what sort of bar this is, huge screens show nonstop NFL matches for your voyeuristic sports pleasure. Of course, a full range of isotonic drinks are available, in addition to beer and cocktails. Two pluses are a reasonably healthy food menu (we sportspeople must maintain the body as a temple) and the incongruous presence of live reggae from time to time (I thought Jamaicans liked a spot of cricket). But hey, no sweat.

Open from 11 a.m. till 4 a.m. every day.
Tokyu Shibuya Beam Bldg. B1F,
31-2 Udagawa-cho,
Shibuya-ku.
(03) 5458-4486
¥

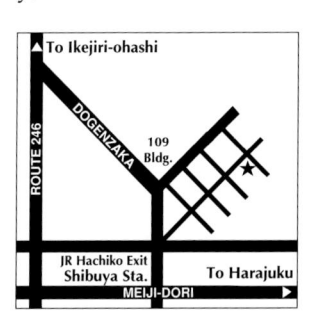

Aspen Glow

This is an extremely friendly and relaxed little bar featuring live music every night. The general clutter of knickknacks and furniture inside instantly tells you that it has been in the same spot for years. A rather undersized bandstand fills one end and a bar dominates the other. In between is a sea of poky little tables and chairs. If you feel like dancing you will usually end up doing so with your knees jammed into some piece of furniture. Depending on the night, you could be entertained with anything from country and western to rockabilly, so check ahead for what's on or take your chances. Any lineup featuring Hi Tide Harris (a regular on Monday) or Keiko Walker (touted as Japan's Emmylou Harris) is guaranteed to be good. But be warned—it is tiny and the *master-san* will keep letting people in until it is unbearable and only then will he turn them away. So if you want to be comfortable you should get there well ahead of showtime. You must order something to eat with your drink.

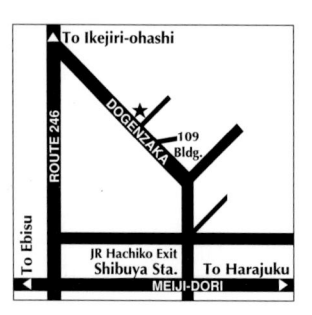

Open from 6:30 p.m. till 12 a.m.
Monday to Saturday. Closed on
Sunday and holidays.
GM Bldg. 6F,
2-28-2 Dogenzaka,
Shibuya-ku.
(03) 3496-9709
¥¥

Rock'n'Roll Diner

There may be times when you might prefer to drink in a slightly more up-market venue than the usual down-home or down and dirty Shimo-kitazawa dives. If so, try the bar overlooking the restaurant in this very popular, retro-50s burger and Tex-mex joint. It is huge inside, but the spatial layout and lighting have been well used to create a pleasantly intimate atmosphere. The decor features lots of chrome railings and red upholstered booths around a central corral of tables. Lots of rock'n'roll memorabilia cover the walls. It is pretty noisy early in the night with groups of gregarious Japanese office workers and preppy-looking English teachers knocking back a few over dinner, but the bar stays open for an hour after the kitchen closes at 11 p.m. Throughout the evening a DJ plays rock classics from one of the most impressive collections of CDs I've spotted. Special deals for live mini-concerts and birthday parties (including a cake and champagne or shooters) are available.

Open from 5 p.m. till 12 a.m.
Sunday to Thursday, and till 2
a.m. on Friday and Saturday.
Big Ben Bldg. B1F,
2-5-2 Kitazawa,
Setagaya-ku.
(03) 3411-6565
¥

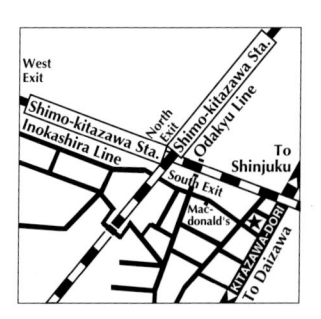

Wild Cards

Rolling Stone

Make sure you take a last gasp of fresh air before descending into the bowels of this hard-core rock dive. The interior looks like it used to be an Italian restaurant complete with red-and-white checkered table cloths and plastic grape vines hanging from the ceiling. The owners obviously decided to save when redecorating, so now instead of Fly Alitalia propaganda, it is wallpapered with Stones' posters and peopled with long-hairs in leather jackets. Tokyo's hard rock and heavy metal subculturalists come here to sit and look mean and sometimes to wait for a fight. There is usually a fairly impressive array of classic Harley Davidsons on the street in front belonging to some of the club's older patrons. Don't be fooled by the sultry mini-skirted waitresses—I've seen them muscle punch-drunk GIs up the stairs without any visible strain on their manicure. The macho volatility ratio rises in direct proportion to the number of customers, which inevitably peaks on the weekend.

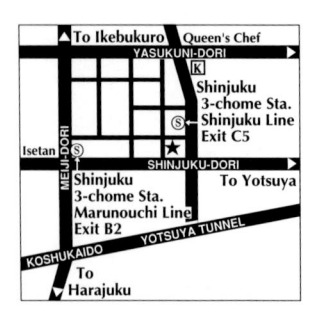

Open from 6 p.m till 4:15 a.m. Monday to Friday, and from 3 p.m. till 4:15 a.m. on Saturday and Sunday.
Ebichu Bldg. B1F,
3-2-7 Shinjuku,
Shinjuku-ku.
(03) 3354-7347
¥

Gag

A pool hall craze erupted in Tokyo several years ago after Tom Cruise's portrayal of a young sharp-shooter in the movie *The Color of Money* (*Hustler II* in Japan). Once the boom died down, many places closed. The management of this bar got rid of all but one of their 12 tables and converted the rest of the space into a *karaoke* bar. For your singing pleasure (or displeasure), there is one large "free" space and several variously-proportioned private rooms. The one remaining pool table is reasonably well-patronized by small groups of expat men, for whom a game of pool is more than just a passing fad. For them it is a pleasant once-a-week after-work relaxant in which they will indulge for the rest of their lives—in much the same way that the Japanese will continue to indulge in *karaoke*. If you want to play pool, it will cost you ¥1,000 to enter and ¥1,000/hour for the table. If you want to sing, the "free" space is available from ¥2,000/head and the private rooms go for ¥5,000/head/two hours.

Open from 7 p.m. till 5 a.m. Monday to Saturday. Closed on Sunday and holidays. New Shinsaka Bldg. B1F, 8-10-22 Akasaka, Minato-ku. (03) 3408-9990 ¥¥/¥¥¥

Wonder Bar

We all know that space is at a premium in Tokyo, and like any city, a lot of this space is given over to sidewalks and roads. Taking advantage of this wasted space, a lateral-thinking party entrepreneur decided to build a free-standing bar on a widish sidewalk in Roppongi. This immediately started a craze for what I call goldfish-bowl bars, which apparently dropped from the heavens like so many UFOs littering the pavement. This one somehow managed to survive the fad and still clings to a side street next to the Roi Building. It has been there almost since the beginning of the craze and, at that time, enjoyed a very robust following. These days it seems to serve more as a meeting place for partygoers bound for points beyond or simply as a venue for that sometimes elusive quiet drink on a Saturday night. You can also watch some of the street's passing parade from the comfort of your barstool. It makes a more pleasant and imagina-tive alternative to meeting at Almond.

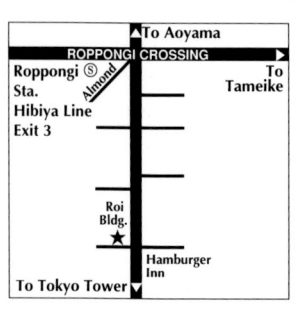

Open from 5 p.m. till 2 a.m.
every day.
Roi Bldg. 1F,
5-5-1 Roppongi,
Minato-ku.
(03) 3423-4666
¥

Paranoia Café

Elm Street relocates in Roppongi with the arrival of this hellhole bar. A giant eyeball glares out malevolently over the top of the building. The stairway is lit with a single black light, which forces you to grope your way up the stairs. The walls are a continuous sea of flesh from which agonized, screaming faces try to tear away from each other. The roof is a festering nest of unblinking eyeballs bearing down on you from seamless pink sockets. One corner houses a tiny cell complete with a closable gate (for more obstreperous customers). Two pets, Dog-foot and Eye-hand, perch unleashed on the bar, while horror movies play nonstop on monitors. But what else would you expect when someone called Screaming Mad George decides to open a bar? He is a Japanese special-effects expert still living in L.A. who has a convincing and decidedly grizzly way with latex. Drinks are a little expensive, but well worth it for the wacky environment. By contrast, all the bar's customers seem quite tame.

Open from 7 p.m. till 2 a.m. Monday to Thursday, and till 4 a.m. on Friday and Saturday. Closed on Sunday. Victory Bldg. 3F, 4-12-5 Roppongi, Minato-ku. (03) 5411-8018 ¥/¥¥

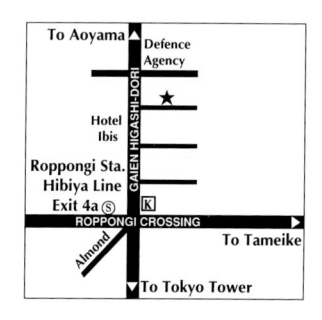

Appendix 1: Yokohama

The low-level urban sprawl that connects Tokyo to Yokohama is a seamless continuum. Except for the fact that central Tokyo is the best part of an hour away by train, there are few clues to let you know that you have arrived in a different city. In fact, this is true of many of Japan's urban centers.

In terms of nightlife, Yokohama could be considered a satellite suburb of Tokyo. Both cities are megalopolises, but they are structured very differently. Their population densities are about the same, with central Tokyo's resident population of eight million spreading out over roughly 1,000 square kilometers and Yokohama's three million occupying just over 400 square kilometers. But what these statistics don't tell you is that Tokyo has many major party centers studded around the city like diamonds in a necklace. Yokohama has only one. So the resulting concentration of clubs in close proximity affords you a more varied and walkable selection of nightlife alternatives.

Over the years, Yokohama has experienced a strong foreign influence due to its proximity to many US bases. This can be a drawback if the lads are out in force and get too boisterous, but the upside is that local proprietors are more used to dealing with foreign faces and tastes. So, with the exception of Circus, the overall scene tends to be more laid-back. The bars and clubs listed here are a random sampling intended to whet your appetite and get you started.

Appendix 1: Yokohama

Brain Club PSY

This is one of the most offbeat bar names I've come across—forget soul train, now there's soul brain. The interior is modern and the music is soulful and funky, which makes it a favorite of mine. It is the only bar in Yokohama that has fliers for parties and events stacked by the door—a sign of being plugged into the scene. Some of them sounded pretty wild, too. This is a cool little bar which deserves to be discovered.

Open from 7 p.m. till 5 a.m. Monday to Saturday, and till 3 a.m. on Sunday and holidays.
Vistalia Motomachi Bldg. B1F, 4-179 Motomachi, Naka-ku.
(045) 641-5865 ¥

Glam Slam

Prince is responsible for the latest version of this club. The entry is a lush and fanciful vestibule worshiping the god of his guitar, the foyer is a small museum of artifacts from his movies, and the interior is clubland at its best—expansive, well-appointed, and plush. Everything has the Prince stamp of approval. The cover charge is expensive, but worth it for the excellent dance music and environment. Get there early on live nights to avoid being stuck behind a pillar.

Open from 6 p.m. till 12 a.m. every day.
3-4 Shin-yamashita, Naka-ku.
(045) 624-3900 ¥¥¥¥

Appendix 1: Yokohama

American House

Welcome to Yokohama's Gaijin Ghetto HQ. It is as unpretentious as its name with predictable American paraphernalia (including a Spud the Bud mascot) tucked into every available corner. It is patronized by a low-key mix of foreigners and locals, but to prevent overcrowding, you must wait for an available bar stool before you can sit and order. It is a decent place to wait for the first train if you can't handle the discos.

Open from 5 p.m. till 2 a.m. Monday to Friday, and from 1 p.m. till 2 a.m. on Saturday and Sunday.
106 Yamashita-cho, Naka-ku.
(045) 681-6780 ¥

Circus

I had been warned about this disco and with good reason. It isn't nightlife. It's wildlife—and it really should be kept in a cage. The signs out front should have put me off—one saying that drunks and rowdies are not allowed and another specifying that all foreigners show ID. Even so, the atmosphere inside is high-volatility sleaze. You get an open bar with entry, but the drinks have never seen a bottle. Everything comes out of a jet and tastes like perfume. Ticky tacky.

Open from 7 p.m. till 3 a.m. or later every day.
Yamashita Bldg. B1F, Yamashita-cho, Naka-ku.
(045) 681-7281/681-7282 ¥¥¥

Appendix 1: Yokohama

Desperado

This is a very quiet neighborhood bar run by a very friendly 40-something Japanese man. He named it after the Eagles' hit and that's what he likes—middle-of-the-road R&B and 70s easy-listening music. The odd party snapshot on the wall indicates that it has more uproarious moments. If I lived in Yokohama, I would develop this as my local (and bring my own music once I got to know the *master* better).

Open from 8 p.m. till 4 a.m. Tuesday to Sunday. Closed on Monday.
1-17 Ishikawa-cho, Naka-ku.
(045) 681-4712 ¥

Laser Rush

An interesting clique of Japanese patronize this low-key video bar. *Genki* boys behind the bar load up the tape deck with reggae and the VCR with box-office movies, which become little more than visual wallpaper if you can't read the subtitles. Most people come here to sit-and-space and don't pay them much attention anyway. The atmosphere is almost introverted, so don't go alone unless that's what you like.

Open from 6 p.m. till 2 a.m. Monday to Saturday. Closed on Sunday and holidays.
1-33 Motomachi, Naka-ku.
(045) 662-5210 ¥

Bar Replay Jr.

Yokohama delivers quality over quantity with this surprisingly sophisticated live jazz venue. But this doesn't mean that it's expensive—there is only a minimal ¥500 music charge. Nor does it mean stuffy—there is a pool table over in one corner, the staff is helpful and friendly, and the overall atmosphere is extremely relaxed. The original Replay is over near Circus, but I don't like that neighborhood.

Open from 5 p.m. till 3 a.m. Monday to Friday, till 3 a.m. or later on Saturday, and from 3 p.m. till 1 a.m. on Sunday and holidays. Labi Motomachi Bldg. 5F, 1-13 Motomachi, Naka-ku. (045) 663-2828 ¥¥

491 House

The existence of this fine establishment directly across the street from Circus puts the latter to shame on every level. Here you can enjoy excellent live jazz delivered by local musicians from the comfort of a wood-paneled booth overlooking the stage. Stained-glass lampshades and ceiling fans complete its warm and slightly retro interior. As with other jazz clubs in Yokohama, there is a minimal ¥500 music charge.

Open from 6 p.m. till 2 a.m. Sunday to Friday, and till 4 a.m. on Saturday.
Tokunaga Bldg. 1F, 82 Yamashita-cho, Naka-ku.
(045) 662-2104 ¥¥

Appendix 2: Late Eats

If you're out on a bender, you may find yourself craving a late-night snack to soak up the alcohol you have consumed. Also, if it is the weekend or a pay day and you miss the last train, getting a taxi can be a viciously competitive situation. During the *bonenkai* and Christmas party season the rivalry for a cab intensifies beyond belief, with rumors of secret hand signals for paying double or triple to drivers running rife. So, if you find yourself stranded with the thought of another drink or crowded bar creating an extremely negative reaction in your stomach, why not hang out in a restaurant until the desperados have thinned out a little? Here are some alternatives to the ever-present *ramen* stand. They are mostly well-positioned restaurant chains that have the after-hours eating market sewn up. Who knows, you may even feel like more partying after a tasty bite to eat.

La Boheme

Reliably good pasta, pizza, and salads.
Open from 11:30 a.m. till 5 a.m. every day. No holidays.
Aoyama (03) 3499-3377, Daikan-yama (03) 3476-4799, Jingumae (03) 3400-3406, Nishi-azabu (03) 3407-1363, Setagaya (03) 5486-1021, Shibuya (03) 3477-0481, Yokohama (045) 662-0901

Sara

Basic European and Japanese food.
Open 24 hours for drinks and from 11 a.m. till 7 a.m. for food every day. No holidays.
Aoyama (03) 3408-8022

Appendix 2: Late Eats

Charleston Cafe Taverna

Up-market Sicilian restaurant with a fanciful interior.
Open from 11:30 a.m. till 4 a.m. Monday to Saturday, and till 11 p.m. on Sunday. Closed for year-end holidays.
Daikanyama (03) 5489-9256

Charleston Son

Tex-Mex, pizza, and hamburger hangout owned by the people who run the bar and Sicilian restaurant of the same name.
Open from 11 a.m. till 4 a.m. Monday to Thursday, till 5 a.m. on Friday and Saturday, and till 3 a.m. on Sunday. Closed for year-end holidays.
Roppongi (03) 3479-0595

Zest

Southern Californian cuisine. The main branch in Jingumae features a very popular pool table.
Open from 12 p.m. till 5 a.m. every day. Jingumae Annex and Yokohama branches open from 5 p.m. till 5 a.m. No holidays.
Jingumae: Main Branch (03) 3409-6268, Annex (03) 3499-0293; Nishi-azabu (03) 3400-3985, Setagaya (03) 5486-0321, Yokohama (045) 662-0941

Ajanta

Good quality Indian food.
Open 24 hours every day. No holidays.
Kojimachi (03) 3264-6955

El Mocambo

Latin-American delicacies served in a trendy Aztec environment.
Open from 6 p.m. till 12 a.m. Monday to Saturday, and till 2 a.m. in December. Closed on Sunday and for year-end holidays.
Nishi-azabu (03) 5410-0468

Appendix 2: Late Eats

Hamburger Inn

Good if you're desperate. As the name suggests, they serve standard American fare, but unfortunately everything is microwaved.

Open from 11:30 p.m. till 5 a.m. Monday to Saturday, and till 2 a.m. on Sunday. Closed on the 2nd and 3rd Sunday of the month and for year-end holidays.
Roppongi (03) 3405-8980

Samrat

Haute Indian cuisine.

Open from 11 a.m. till 5 a.m. every day. Closed for year-end holidays.
Roppongi (03) 3478-5877, Shibuya Pub (03) 3770-7275, Shinjuku (03) 3355-1533

Ban Tai

Delicious Thai food.

Open from 11:30 a.m. till 3 p.m. for lunch and from 5 p.m. till 12 a.m. for dinner Monday to Friday, and continuously from 11:30 a.m. till 12 a.m. on Saturday and Sunday. Closed for year-end holidays.
Shinjuku (03) 3207-0068

Garlic Chips

Tasty garlic dishes and a wide range of bourbon.

Open from 11 p.m. till 3 a.m. Monday to Saturday. Closed on Sunday.
Takada-no-baba (03) 3232-1490

Glossary

Note: Japanized English words are written using Western romanizations (otherwise you wouldn't recognize them).

ai-seki	sharing a table with people you don't know
aka-cho-chin	red lantern indicating a small, traditional eating and drinking spot
bonenkai	obligatory end-of-year drinking binge
bottle-keep	bottle bought by you and kept at a bar until you finish it (or forget it)
fundoshi	traditional Japanese loincloth
gaijin	you if you're not Japanese (them if you are)
genki	happy, hale, hearty, and able to party
gomi	trash
happi	short cotton kimono worn at festivals
Homat	housing company specializing in plush, oversized expat apartments
ikebana	traditional Japanese flower arrangement
karaoke	sing-along only enjoyed by the person with the mike (but everyone applauds)
koban	small, neighborhood police station (to be avoided without your *gaijin* card)
lock'n'loll	rock'n'roll, stupid
mama, mama-san	she who owns the booze
master, master-san	he who owns the booze
mingei	traditional Japanese arts and crafts
mini-komi	underground or minor market
new-half	having lost your sex to the scalpel

Glossary

nomiya	drinking spot or pub
odenya	shop selling smelly, rubbery stew
oishii	delicious, tasty (even if it isn't)
okyakusan	you if you're ordering, them if you're serving
OL	acronym for Office Lady, which translates as secretary or tea maker
oshibori	hot or cold hand towel brought to you when you enter or leave a bar (possibly last used at a soapland)
otsumami	light snack
plus alpha	a little extra for a lot more money
ramen	Chinese noodles
sakura	young couple hired by a club to break the ice on the dance floor
salaryman	male company employee
Shibu-kaji	abbreviation of Shibuya casual refering to the mobs of teenagers hanging out in Shibuya looking like they should be trout fishing instead
shinjinrui	Japan's new generation regarded as rude, selfish, and inconsiderate (but really they're just a whole lot of fun)
snack	small drinking spot usually run by an older woman who acts as hostess
Takarazuka	famous, glitzy, all-female theater group notorious for having young female groupies
yakitoriya	restaurant selling tasty barbecued chicken bits on a stick
yellow cab	Japanese woman interested in foreign men who is as easy to pick up as a cab in New York

Club Index

Club Index

Club/Area Index

Area Index

Area Index

Area Index